Idaho Twelvers

A Hiking Guide For Idaho's Nine Peaks Over 12,000 Feet

Idaho Twelvers

A Hiking Guide For Idaho's Nine Peaks Over 12,000 Feet

by Ryan Byers

 Lost River Publishing LLC

> **WARNING!** Mountaineering is an inherently dangerous activity. Every route in this book contains a measure of risk. The users of this guidebook assume full responsibility for their own safety. While effort has been made to make the trail descriptions as accurate as possible, there may be discrepancies between the text and the actual trails. Routes change from day to day and season to season. Do not rely solely on the information in this book for your safety. This book cannot replace experience, sound judgment, and good decision-making. Prepare for the unexpected and be cautious. And remember, the mountain will always be there, but you will not. Never be afraid to turn around and attempt the mountain another day.

Idaho Twelvers: A Hiking Guide For Idaho's Nine Peaks Over 12,000 Feet
© 2023 Ryan Byers

Photos and cover design: Ryan Byers
Interior and map design: Ryan Byers
Topo and satellite map imagery: Customaps.com
Editor: Mary Byers
Cover image: Rob Kleffner descending Leatherman Peak

International Standard Book Number: 979-8-9876471-0-3
Library of Congress Control Number: 2023901358

First Edition. Updated in 2024.
Published by Lost River Publishing LLC
lostriverpublishing.com

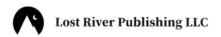 **Lost River Publishing LLC**

*To my parents, Steve and Mary,
for encouraging my brother and me to explore
the wilderness from a young age.*

Borah Peak from the south.

Contents

Preface

From the first time I climbed Borah Peak in 2011, I was hooked on mountaineering. I found the experience overwhelming and exhausting, but also incredibly profound. It unlocked a drive in me that few activities have ever been able to replicate. Watching the glow of the early morning sun light up the ragged peaks while pausing to catch one's breath is otherworldly.

When I discovered Borah was just one of Idaho's nine 12,000ft peaks, I became obsessed with climbing the rest of them. I had difficulty finding reliable information about the routes on these other peaks and often found myself in dangerous terrain, which inspired me to write this book. My goal with this book is to provide a resource valuable to any climber. Between trail descriptions, GPS waypoints, topo/satellite maps, and elevation profiles, there hopefully will be something of value in here for those who, like me, must inexplicably climb these mountains.

Acknowledgments

Creating a book is a massive undertaking, and I appreciate everyone in my life for allowing me to constantly ask for feedback on my writing, photo selection, and design choices. I would also like to thank everyone who has joined me in the mountains over the years. Every hike is a new chance to learn, and I value spending time with others in the mountains.

I want to thank Rob Kleffner, Daniel Wells, Adria Mead, Sara Goodwin, and my family, Mary, Steve, and John Byers, among countless others, for helping me get this edition of the book out.

idahotwelvers.com

If you notice anything on the trails that is different than in this book, I would love to hear about it! Visit **idahotwelvers.com** to submit feedback so that future editions of this book are as trail-accurate as possible. The website has GPX files of each peak for even more assistance in the mountains. Several Twelver items are also available to purchase, including t-shirts, stickers, magnets, and more.

Idaho Twelvers Map

Pioneer Mountains

1. Hyndman Peak
   (12,009 feet)

Lost River Range

2. Borah Peak
   (12,662 feet)

3. Mount Idaho
   (12,065 feet)

4. Leatherman Peak
   (12,228 feet)

5. Mount Church
   (12,200 feet)

6. Donaldson Peak
   (12,023 feet)

7. Mount Breitenbach
   (12,140 feet)

8. Lost River Peak
   (12,078 feet)

Lemhi Range

9. Diamond Peak
   (12,197 feet)

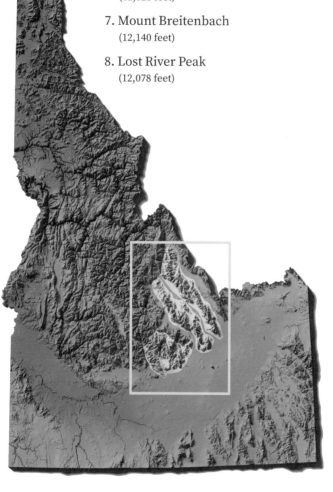

Introduction

Borah Peak, Idaho's towering state highpoint, attracts thousands of intrepid climbers each year daring to reach its rocky summit and earn bragging rights. While most who make it up this 12,662ft giant have their summit itch scratched, others crave more. For these inspired hikers, Idaho's nine 12,000ft peaks, or "Twelvers," have become an increasingly popular challenge.

Summiting these peaks is no simple feat though. The wide variety of routes, lack of established trails, harsh terrain, and conflicting information online can overwhelm new climbers. The purpose of this book is to help climbers, both beginners and experienced mountaineers, to summit each of the nine Twelvers using standard routes. Each mountain has been researched, photographed, and climbed multiple times by the author. Maps, GPS coordinates, photos, route descriptions, and everything else in this book are designed to make the chances of a successful summit as high as possible.

The Twelvers

The nine mountains in Idaho over 12,000 feet in elevation offer hikers a chance to test their mental and physical limits. The varying terrain encountered on each mountain provides unique challenges to those who dare attempt them. Overgrown creeks, endless screebowls, and exposed scrambles along cliff edges, where one mistake could lead to falling through the air hundreds of feet, will test those who set out to conquer these mountains. Those who make it to the summits are rewarded with an incredible sense of accomplishment. For some, it's the breathtaking views, and for others, the satisfaction of knowing they pushed themselves past their limits.

Borah Peak from the northwest.

Idaho's Twelvers are split between three mountain ranges: the Pioneer Mountains, the Lost River Range, and the Lemhi Range. The vast majority of these peaks, including the Idaho highpoint Borah Peak, are located in the Lost River Range. Each one of these peaks ends with a steep climb on crumbling rocks. Some, such as Leatherman Peak and Hyndman Peak, offer gradual segments through scenic terrain. Others, like Lost River Peak, throw hikers directly onto the steep slopes. Each of the peaks requires some form of route finding. Be prepared to navigate without a defined hiking trail.

The nine peaks are listed below, from highest to lowest.

Mountain Name	Elevation	Range
Borah Peak	12,662 feet	Lost River Range
Leatherman Peak	12,228 feet	Lost River Range
Mount Church	12,200 feet	Lost River Range
Diamond Peak	12,197 feet	Lemhi Range
Mount Breitenbach	12,140 feet	Lost River Range
Lost River Peak	12,078 feet	Lost River Range
Mount Idaho	12,065 feet	Lost River Range
Donaldson Peak	12,023 feet	Lost River Range
Hyndman Peak	12,009 feet	Pioneer Mountains

The difficulty of these peaks is highly subjective. Each mountain has obstacles that test hikers in different ways. For instance, Borah's Chicken Out Ridge may be an enjoyable, stress-free experience for some, but it can be an impenetrable obstacle for others. Some may have no difficulty navigating trail-less creek beds, but others may become disoriented and have to call it quits.

Author's Note
If you are new to scrambling and need a starter Twelver, I recommend Hyndman Peak. It has a beautiful and well-marked approach with a good taste of scrambling on the summit.

Those who successfully summit each of the nine Twelvers become part of a small but proud group of hikers. You can add your name to the ever-growing list at **idahotwelvers.com.**

Using This Book

The mountains in this book are divided by mountain range, from west to east. When multiple peaks are located within the same range, they are listed from north to south.

Overview: A general description of what to expect from the mountain.

Climbing Route: The route name, usually named after the ridge used to summit. Unless otherwise noted, the routes listed in this book are the standard and least difficult way to summit these peaks. Other routes exist for each mountain, but are not featured in this book due to the difficulty and technicality required to ascend them.

Rating: The Yosemite Decimal System (YDS) rating, from Class 1 to 5, of a route. Difficulty is subjective, so consider your strengths and weaknesses when planning a hike.

Elevation Gain: The total elevation gained during a climb. This number takes into account the ups and downs that occur throughout the hike, not just the difference between summit and trailhead altitudes.

Round Trip Time and Distance: The estimated time and distance to summit and return to the trailhead for a reasonably fit hiker. Will vary significantly based on individual fitness level and the number of hikers in a group (the more people there are, the slower the pace will be).

Water: If a water source such as a creek or pond is available on the route. Bring a water filter if you decide to drink from these sources. Untreated water can contain bacteria and protozoa such as giardia, cryptosporidium, and salmonella.

Maps: The included maps display the routes on both contour and satellite imagery. In addition to the maps, each route also lists the United States Geological Survey (USGS) 7.5-minute maps, and the United States Forest Service (USFS) maps that apply to the area.

Name: The origin of a mountain's name.

First Ascent: The first known person to successfully climb to the summit.

Nearest Town: The closest location to the trailhead where gas, food, and lodging can be found unless otherwise noted.

Prominence: The height of a mountain relative to the lowest contour line encircling the mountain that does not have a higher summit within it.

Getting There: Driving instructions to reach the trailhead. For the mountains in the Lost River Range, the initial odometer distances are measured starting from the Lost River Ranger District Office (716 Custer St, Mackay, Idaho).

Route Description: The detailed trail guide. Orange text denotes GPS waypoints.

Elevation Profile: A visual representation of the route using elevation and distance to form a graph.

GPS Coordinates: The coordinates for notable waypoints on the route. Displayed as Degrees and Decimal Minutes DDD° MM.MMM'

▶ **GPS Coordinates, Elevation Listings, Distances, and Safety:** Throughout the book, you will see various elevation/distance markings and GPS waypoints meant to help keep you on the route during your climb. However, GPS reliability can be affected by satellite positioning, atmospheric conditions, receiver quality, and signal-blocking terrain (cliff walls, tree coverage, etc.). Similarly, changing weather patterns can also affect barometric devices that use air pressure to measure altitude. I mention this to say that while technology is beneficial, be prepared to navigate each hike using trail descriptions and on-sight route finding.

Climbing Ratings

Yosemite Decimal System Class ratings are determined by grading the difficulty of the most technically difficult portion of a climb, and assessing the technique used to ascend it. The hardest part of the climb is also referred to as the crux. It is important to remember that the overall difficulty of the route may be different than the rating. For example, a four-mile hike with constant Class 3 terrain may very well be more taxing than a two-mile hike with a small section of Class 4 climbing.

Class 1: A maintained hiking trail. Little to no exposure.

Class 2: A rough hiking trail with some exposure that may require use of hands for balancing, such as crossing a large field of boulders. Route finding may be required.

Class 3: Steep scrambling with moderate exposure that requires the use of handholds to progress. Falls could lead to serious injury or death.

Class 4: Steep scrambling and minor rock climbing with severe exposure. Falls may be fatal. Ropes are often used during sections of the hike.

Class 5: Technical rock climbing. Ropes and anchors are needed to ascend safely. Only experienced rock climbers should attempt these routes.

The + symbol means the rating is more difficult than average.

When To Climb

Time of Year

The optimal climbing season for all the routes in this book is from late July to early September. During these summer months, the weather will be more stable, and the trails mostly snow-free. **For beginners, August is an excellent month to venture out into these mountains.**

Climbing earlier in the season, from late spring to early summer, may require snow and ice gear. Climbing after Labor Day is weather dependent. Some years you can climb well into October with no snow, while other years, snow may fall by the end of September. A light dusting of snow late in the season might not seem like a problem, but it could lead to the existence of ice on the route, which can be incredibly dangerous, especially on the exposed parts of the route where you may be climbing on bare rock.

Time of Day

The optimal time of day to start a climb is before sunrise. Beginning in the dark, also called an "Alpine Start," gives climbers a chance to summit and get off the exposed upper mountain before afternoon thunderstorms move in. Alpine Starts can also keep you away from crowded late-morning trailheads.

What To Bring

Hiking can bring out a variety of personal tastes when it comes to gear selection. One hiker's kit might be a non-starter for another. Instead of listing specific items, a more modern approach is to list the type of items to bring.

1. **Hydration** - Water and/or water filtration. Electrolyte drinks and powders are encouraged.

2. **Nutrition** - Having too much food is better than not having enough. A mixture of proteins and complex carbohydrates is a good choice.

3. **Insulation** - Be prepared for a variety of weather conditions. At the very

least, bring a waterproof layer, gloves, a warm hat, and a light jacket.

4. **Illumination** - A headlamp or flashlight. Don't rely on just a smartphone for light. Extra batteries are essential.

5. **First Aid** - A general-purpose first aid kit to help you or others in emergencies.

6. **Sun Protection** - Light sunproof layers, sunscreen, SPF lip balm, sunglasses, and a hat.

7. **Fire Starters** - Waterproof matches or weatherproof fire starters.

8. **Emergency Shelter** - Emergency blanket or bivy.

9. **Repair Kit** - Duct tape, multitool, knife, extra pack buckles, etc.

10. **Navigation** - A map, compass, or GPS. Something to provide location information.

Author's Note

An item that always goes into my backpack on these hikes is a canister of bear spray. While the chances of needing it are very slim, it never hurts to be prepared.

Mountaineering-specific items - **trekking poles, climbing gloves, and climbing helmets** are encouraged. Hiking up and down thousands of feet in a single hike can be brutal on the knees. Trekking poles can help alleviate this stress and provide balance and assistance while moving on precarious terrain. Climbing gloves protect the hands from the sharp rock on ridge scrambles. Climbing helmets are always a good idea on these rockfall-prone mountains.

As for more technical gear like **climbing ropes, ice axes, crampons, etc.,** the standard routes listed in this book are all non-technical, meaning you shouldn't need any specialized gear to reach the summits during the regular season.

▶ **A possible exception to this is Borah Peak.** Right after Chicken Out Ridge, there is a snow bridge that usually melts by the end of the summer. For the majority of people climbing in the summer, even when the snow bridge is there, technical gear is not needed to cross this obstacle safely. If you are nervous about traversing this section, **ice cleats / microspikes** are a cheap and lightweight option that wrap around most hiking footwear and provide traction on snow and ice. When paired with hiking poles, they provide a solid option for traversing this section.

Camping, Lodging, Parking and Permits

Camping

The only Twelver trailhead with a dedicated campground is Borah Peak (which has a small fee). The rest of the trailheads and routes are on Forest Service land, which allows dispersed camping (camping outside of designated campsites; 16-day limit). If you do choose to camp, try and set up 100 feet away from any creek. Also keep in mind that you are in black bear country, so store food accordingly.

Most climbers on these peaks sleep at the trailhead the night before the climb, either in a tent or in their vehicle. This allows them to begin the hike minutes after they wake up, saving precious morning time. If you choose to camp at the trailheads, be prepared for chilly nights on rocky and uneven ground. Also, be considerate of noise and light when setting up camp or gearing up for the hike.

Lodging

While the preferred method for most hikers is camping at the trailhead, others may prefer the comfort of a soft bed and a shower. For Hyndman Peak, lodging is available nearby in Hailey and Ketchum, Idaho. For the Lost River Range peaks, Mackay, Idaho, offers a variety of accommodations. Diamond Peak is the only mountain with no local lodging. Arco and Idaho Falls, Idaho, are both options for those looking to stay in a hotel before climbing Diamond Peak.

Parking and Permits

Climbers are fortunate because none of the peaks require permits or parking passes to climb. Hyndman Peak and Borah Peak are the only two trailheads with some sort of dedicated parking area. Both of those are also the only two with camp toilets. For the rest of the mountains, be prepared to park on uneven hillsides just off the road.

Mountain Hazards

Mountain climbing is inherently a dangerous activity. The very nature of the sport places climbers in precarious situations in unforgiving terrain. While the vast majority of hikers heading out into the mountains will run into no trouble, it is important to be aware of potential dangers and how to avoid them.

Lightning

Lightning is a genuine concern when mountaineering. Afternoon thunderstorms are common in the mountains and can put climbers at risk if they are on exposed terrain.

▶ Lightning may be visible if a storm is around 15 miles away. If you can hear the thunder, that means the storm is closer, likely under ten miles away. To calculate the distance, count how long it takes in seconds for the thunder boom to sound after the flash appears. Divide that number by five to estimate miles.

▶ Start hiking early in the morning to lower your chance of encountering lightning. Be off the exposed upper mountain before afternoon cumulus clouds have the opportunity to move in. Be sure to check weather forecasts before beginning a climb.

▶ Even with the best preparation and planning, a sudden storm can still sneak up on you.

▽ If caught in a lightning storm, move downhill as soon as possible.

▽ Try to seek shelter in a forest among a low stand of trees.

▽ When on the upper mountain, avoid shallow caves and overhangs, as they will not provide protection from side flashes (lightning moving laterally on the ground in poor conductivity areas).

▽ Avoid open meadows, ridges, summits, bodies of water, and isolated trees. Avoid being the tallest object in an area. If hiking in a group, spread out by 50 yards and squat on the balls of your feet.

Author's Note

During my first ascent of Lost River Peak, a lightning storm abruptly snuck up on my friend and me in the morning. We quickly hurried to a nearby stand of trees and hunkered down on the balls of our feet. I will never forget the terror I felt as the lightning cracked down just yards away from us. The storm eventually passed and we walked away unharmed, but the experience has never left me. Be vigilant in watching the weather as you climb, especially as you leave the safety of the tree line.

Rockfall

Seasonal thawing of ice in the steep talus and scree fields creates fresh opportunities for rockfall every year. Given that the routes up every one of the mountains in this book pass through this terrain, it is important to prepare for the rocky hazards that await.

▶ Wear a helmet.

▶ When climbing with a group, stay very close together so that dislodged rocks may be sidestepped. If staying in close proximity is not possible, avoid climbing directly below others while in loose terrain. Coordinate movements so that the higher climbers are not dropping rocks on anyone below them.

▶ Listen for rockfall above and be prepared to move out of danger.

▶ If you dislodge a rock or see one on the move, yell "Rock!" to alert others of the danger.

▶ When scrambling, be sure to carefully test handholds to prevent pulling rocks out onto either yourself or those below you.

▶ **NEVER throw a rock**, especially on a summit. What may look like a barren cliff to you may in fact be an alternate route that has climbers hundreds of feet below out of view.

Author's Note

In almost every scenario, climbing with another person makes hiking a safer experience. However, hiking near others can be dangerous when climbing up steep rockfall-prone terrain. While hiking Granite Peak in Montana, a massive boulder my friend was standing on suddenly became dislodged and tumbled down a narrow gully toward another hiker. My group yelled "Rock!" and alerted the hiker, who just narrowly jumped out of the way before the boulder could reach him. While the hiker was alive, he injured his ankle from the last-second dodge, preventing him from progressing any further. With hiking being such a remote activity, working together and communicating is an ideal way to keep the experience safer for everyone.

Avalanches

Climbing the Twelvers during their normal climbing season (July - September), when the snowpack is slim to none, keeps the vast majority of hikers out of avalanche danger. However, those who choose to climb in the winter or spring need to be aware of the very real potential for avalanches on these routes. This is especially true of Lost River Peak, as the mountain is becoming increasingly popular to climb during the late spring.

Lost River Peak from the southwest.

That said, avalanches are a complex topic that is beyond the scope of this book. If you are interested in climbing these mountains during the off-season, I recommend researching avalanches and snow conditions as much as possible, as well as purchasing avalanche safety gear.

Snow

Avalanches are not the only way for snow to pose a threat. In addition to being slick, snow can hide deep pits and loose boulders. Glissading, a method of sledding downhill on snow using an ice axe or a pole, should only be attempted by those with experience. If climbing when snow is unavoidable on the route, make sure you have the gear to circumvent it properly.

Altitude

At 12,000 feet, you will be breathing in 40% fewer oxygen molecules per breath than if you were at sea level. The effect this has on the body varies from person to person. Some people experience fatigue and have difficulty catching their breath. Acute Mountain Sickness (AMS), is a step beyond those symptoms and is categorized as the following:

▶ **Mild to Moderate AMS:** Headache, dizziness, nausea, rapid heart rate, difficulty sleeping, loss of appetite, and swelling of hands, feet, and face.

▶ **Severe AMS:** Vomiting, unable to catch a breath while resting, confusion, and tightening in the chest. If you experience severe symptoms, immediately descend to a lower altitude. In rare cases, severe AMS can progress into HACE or HAPE, both life-threatening.

▽ **HACE** (High-altitude cerebral edema) is fluid entering and putting pressure on the brain.

▽ **HAPE** (High-altitude pulmonary edema) is a buildup of excess fluid in the lungs.

Being physically and cardiovascularly fit, while incredibly useful for the hike itself, is no guarantee for preventing altitude sickness. It can strike all types of hikers, seemingly at random, even those who have been at high altitudes and unaffected previously. Hikers from sea level and lower elevations are especially vulnerable to its effects.

So what can you do to prevent it? Acclimating, the process of spending days at a specific elevation to let the body adjust to that altitude before moving higher, is not a practical method for most people when climbing the Twelvers. Instead, staying hydrated is the next best way to prepare your body for high altitude. Drink plenty of water, both before and during the hike. Avoid alcohol and smoking. Take plenty of breaks.

Hydration

Hydrating throughout the hike is essential to replace the sweat lost through exercise and to minimize the effect altitude has on your body. Aim to drink 16-24 ounces of water per hour. Electrolyte packets take up little space in a pack and are great for keeping you hydrated. If you are drinking caffeine, which can help energy levels at altitude, be sure to compensate for the slight dehydration that it causes. Also, instead of consuming large amounts of water all at once, drink smaller amounts more frequently. Failing to stay hydrated can lead to heat exhaustion.

▶ **Heat Exhaustion:** When the body overheats and cannot cool down, typically through excessive sweating. Symptoms include:

▽ Heavy sweating	▽ Clammy skin
▽ Dizziness	▽ Nausea and vomiting
▽ Fatigue	▽ Weak pulse

Energy

Mountaineering is an energy heavy expenditure. A typical climber will burn anywhere from 300 to 600 calories per hour. While you shouldn't expect to fully replenish every spent calorie during the hike, at least bring enough nutritious snacks to keep your body running efficiently. Altitude and exhaustion can affect what your stomach and taste buds agree on, so a wide variety of snacks, such as granola bars, fruit snacks, and nuts, is recommended.

Temperature and Weather

Between shifting weather and gaining elevation (the temperature drops three to six degrees Fahrenheit for every 1,000 feet of elevation gained,) be prepared to deal with fluctuating temperatures. Mornings can start out cold but quickly become scorchers, and vice versa. Weather can rapidly change on a mountain. Summits and exposed ridges are notorious for relentless wind. Bring a variety of clothing to be prepared. Keep an eye out for the following:

▶ **Hypothermia:** When your body loses heat faster than it can produce it, you are at risk for hypothermia. Symptoms include:

▽ Shivering   ▽ Memory loss

▽ Exhaustion   ▽ Slurred speech

▽ Confusion   ▽ Drowsiness

▽ Fumbling hands

▶ **Frostbite:** Damage to the skin and underlying tissue due to exposure to cold and freezing. Symptoms include:

▽ A white or grayish-yellow skin area

▽ Skin that feels unusually firm or waxy

▽ Numbness

Wildlife

Every trail in this book passes through black bear, mountain lion, and wolf country. While the chances of encountering these elusive predators are slim, it never hurts to be informed on how to deal with them.

▶ **Black Bears:** Smaller and less aggressive than grizzly bears, black bears are timid around humans. If surprised by a hiker, they are likely to flee or hide in a tree instead of attack. When black bear attacks happen, they tend to be predatory, meaning they are looking at humans as food. The standard "play dead" advice does not apply to predatory attacks. If a black bear attacks you, fight back with everything you can. Aim for the face and muzzle.

▶ **Mountain Lions:** The same advice for black bears applies to mountain lions, also known as cougars. Fight back if attacked. If you are stalked, maintain eye contact and make yourself appear as large as possible.

▶ **Wolves:** You are incredibly unlikely to see these large canines on these mountains, but if you encounter one, make yourself look as large as possible. Maintain eye contact and back away slowly. Fight back if attacked.

With all of these animals, making yourself known on the trail, especially when approaching blind turns, can help prevent an encounter. If you are ever forced to engage with one of these animals, a canister of bear spray is an excellent deterrent. If you choose to hike with a canister, ensure it is readily available to deal with aggressive wildlife immediately.

A couple more animals found in these areas may cause trouble for hikers.

▶ **Moose**: These massive herbivores generally stay out of the way of humans, but they can become aggressive if they feel threatened. If you see a moose, give it a wide amount of space. If you are charged by one, seek shelter, such as behind a solid tree.

▶ **Rattlesnakes:** While they are uncommon on these mountains, it is possible to encounter them, especially at lower elevations such as the trailheads. Be careful lifting objects that may shelter them, such as fallen trees or large boulders. If you encounter one rattling, carefully back away from it and give it plenty of space. Leave them alone and they will leave you alone. If bitten, descend the mountain and seek medical attention immediately.

Two other animals worth mentioning in this book purely for viewing awareness are **Mountain Goats** and **Bighorn Sheep**. These high-altitude climbers thrive in the cliffy terrain that all the Twelver summits occupy. Mountain goats, white with small pointed horns, can be found in the Lemhi Range and the Pioneer Mountains. Bighorn sheep, tan with large horns, can be found in the Pioneer Mountains, Lost River Range, and the Lemhi Range.

Keep your distance from every animal in these mountains! After all, this is their home; you are just visiting it.

Cell Service

Cell service is non-existent for many of these hikes and should never be relied upon. Always tell another person where you are going and when you can be expected to return before you set out on the trail. Provide as much information as possible, including the mountain name, route description, number of people in your party, etc., in the event a rescue party is needed.

Deaths

There have been seven hiking-related deaths on the Twelvers, four of which have occurred on Borah Peak. In 1954, a climber was killed by lightning while descending near Borah's summit. In November of 1977, two climbers were killed by an avalanche while attempting the Northwest Ridge route. The most recent death on Borah was in June of 1987 when a climber died in an avalanche after losing control of his glissade.

Mount Church and Donaldson Peak are the locations of two deaths on the Twelvers. In August of 2006, two climbers made a wrong turn on Mount Church and Donaldson Peak's then-standard route up the South Fork of Jones Creek. They turned up the wrong scree field and wound up in Class 5 terrain, where one hiker fell over 150 feet to their death. In May of 2024, a skier died in an avalanche on Donaldson Peak.

Over in the Lemhi Range, a climber died on Diamond Peak in September of 2018 after falling off the mountainside on a dangerous stretch of the climb.

Author's Note

In 2018, a friend and I made the same wrong turn on Mount Church that those climbers did back in 2006. We turned off the creek and made it up several hundred feet until we reached rugged Class 5 terrain. At that point, we realized we were likely off route and descended back to the creek. We found the real path and resumed the hike. Having seen how easy it is to make a potentially life-threatening turn on the South Fork of Jones Creek, I have decided not to include that route in this book. The North Fork route listed in this book is more straightforward, better marked, and a more leisurely hike than the South Fork anyway, so deciding which route to include was simple.

Wildflowers in Hyndman Basin.

Cushion Buckwheat on Hyndman Peak.

Climber Etiquette

When out on the trails, knowing the following set of hiking rules helps decrease confusion and keeps the experience friendly for all:

▶ Hikers moving uphill have the right of way. If you are descending and come in contact with a group ascending, step aside and let them pass by. An uphill hiker might step aside and let a downhill party continue, but that is the uphill hiker's call.

  ▽ An exception to this is when an obvious turnoff is next to the trail. In situations like this, the party with access to the turnoff yields the right of way.

▶ Hike single file to prevent damaging the trailside vegetation.

▶ If a single hiker comes across a group, the single hiker will yield to the group.

▶ When approaching another hiker from behind, make your presence known ahead of time in a calm way. A friendly "hi" will do just fine. Nobody likes a jump scare in the mountains.

Leave No Trace

With the ever-increasing amount of people heading out into the Idaho wilderness, we must strive to help preserve and maintain these environments for everyone to enjoy. Leave No Trace, a nonprofit organization whose core principles were built in collaboration with the U.S. Forest Service, National Park Service, and Bureau of Land Management, has developed seven principles to help minimize our outdoor impact. These principles are:

1. **Plan Ahead and Prepare**

   ▶ Know the regulations and special concerns for the area you'll visit.

   ▶ Prepare for extreme weather, hazards, and emergencies.

   ▶ Schedule your trip to avoid times of high use.

   ▶ Visit in small groups when possible. Consider splitting larger groups into smaller groups.

   ▶ Repackage food to minimize waste.

   ▶ Use a map and compass or GPS to eliminate the use of marking paint, rock cairns or flagging.

2. **Travel and Camp on Durable Surfaces**

   ▶ Durable surfaces include maintained trails and designated campsites, rock, gravel, sand, dry grasses or snow.

   ▶ Protect riparian areas by camping at least 200 feet from lakes and streams.

   ▶ Good campsites are found, not made. Altering a site is not necessary.

   ▽ In popular areas:

   ⊙ Concentrate use on existing trails and campsites.

   ⊙ Walk single file in the middle of the trail, even when wet or muddy.

   ⊙ Keep campsites small. Focus activity in areas where vegetation is absent.

   ▽ In pristine areas:

   ⊙ Disperse use to prevent the creation of campsites and trails.

   ⊙ Avoid places where impacts are just beginning.

3. **Dispose of Waste Properly**

   ▶ Pack it in, pack it out. Inspect your campsite, food preparation areas, and rest areas for trash or spilled foods. Pack out all trash, leftover food and litter.

   ▶ Utilize toilet facilities whenever possible. Otherwise, deposit solid human waste in catholes dug six to eight inches deep, at least 200 feet from water, camp and trails. Cover and disguise the cathole when finished.

   ▶ Pack out toilet paper and hygiene products.

   ▶ To wash yourself or your dishes, carry water 200 feet away from streams or lakes and use small amounts of biodegradable soap. Scatter strained dishwater.

4. **Leave What You Find**

   ▶ Preserve the past: examine, photograph, but do not touch cultural or historic structures and artifacts.

   ▶ Leave rocks, plants and other natural objects as you find them.

   ▶ Avoid introducing or transporting non-native species.

   ▶ Do not build structures, furniture, or dig trenches.

5. **Minimize Campfire Impacts**

   ▶ Campfires can cause lasting impacts to the environment. Use a lightweight stove for cooking and enjoy a candle lantern for light.

   ▶ Where fires are permitted, use established fire rings, fire pans, or mound fires.

   ▶ Keep fires small. Only use down and dead wood from the ground that can be broken by hand.

   ▶ Burn all wood and coals to ash, put out campfires completely, then scatter cool ashes.

6. **Respect Wildlife**

   ▶ Observe wildlife from a distance. Do not follow or approach them.

   ▶ Never feed animals. Feeding wildlife damages their health, alters natural behaviors, (habituates them to humans), and exposes them to predators and other dangers.

   ▶ Protect wildlife and your food by storing rations and trash securely.

- ► Control pets at all times, or leave them at home.
- ► Avoid wildlife during sensitive times: mating, nesting, raising young, or winter.

7. **Be Considerate of Other Visitors**

- ► Respect other visitors and protect the quality of their experience.
- ► Be courteous. Yield to other users on the trail.
- ► Step to the downhill side of the trail when encountering pack stock.
- ► Take breaks and camp away from trails and other visitors.
- ► Let nature's sounds prevail. Avoid loud voices and noises.

©Leave No Trace: www.LNT.org

Mount Morrison from Borah Peak.

A Final Word

Attempting these mountains requires knowledge and attributes that cannot be obtained from this book alone. These hikes are physically demanding. Hiking up 5,000 feet in just a few miles is tough on the body. A solid physical base, especially aerobically, is essential. Be ready to hike for over 10+ hours. It is also important to remember that reaching the summit is just the halfway point, not the end. A successful summit requires making it back to the trailhead safely. Don't spend all your energy making it just one way.

Being mentally prepared also cannot be understated. Weather can turn. Routes can change. Emergencies can happen. How you react to these situations can determine if you will live or die. Do not force yourself into situations or terrain that you feel unprepared for. Never let a route description, GPS heading, or anything else in this book convince you to enter dangerous terrain you are not comfortable with.

And remember, there is never any shame in turning around before the top. The summit will always be waiting for you another day.

Rock cairn on Mount Idaho.

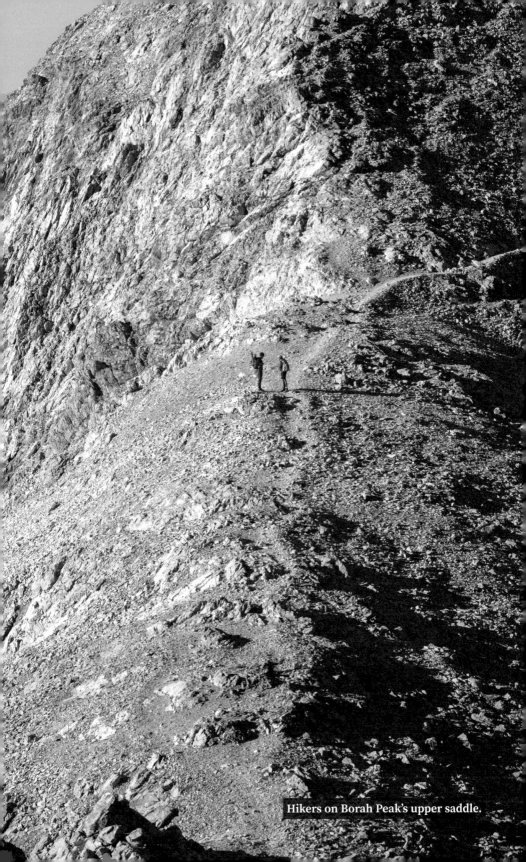

Hikers on Borah Peak's upper saddle.

Pioneer Mountains

The Pioneer Range, located in Central Idaho, runs northwest to southeast for 50 miles, from Ketchum to Arco. While the range is only home to one Twelver, it has many other magnificent summits in pristine glacially carved U-valleys. The name of the range comes from the pioneers that settled the area.

Old Hyndman Peak and Cobb Peak above Hyndman Basin.

Hyndman Peak from the southwest.

Hyndman Peak

12,009 feet (3,660 meters)

9th Highest Twelver

Climbing Route: East Ridge
Rating: Class 2+
Elevation Gain: 5,000 feet
Round Trip Distance: 13 miles
Round Trip Time: 9 hours
Water: Water can be easily found in the various creeks and ponds until just before the saddle
Map: USGS: Hyndman Peak, U.S. Forest Service: Salmon-Challis - Challis (east), U.S. Forest Service: Sawtooth National Forest Ketchum Fairfield South

Name: Named after Major William Hyndman, a Civil War veteran, lawyer, and miner of the Wood River area during the 1880s
First Ascent: First ascent was by USGS topographers W.T. Griswold and E.T. Perkins in 1889
Nearest Town: Hailey, ID
Prominence: 4,810 feet (1,466 meters)

Overview

The hike up Idaho's shortest Twelver is arguably the most scenic on the list. In particular, Hyndman Basin is striking, as this high alpine meadow covered in wildflowers sits below three towering mountains; Hyndman Peak, Old Hyndman Peak, and Cobb Peak. While the hike is a good choice for beginning mountaineers, the long length, exposed summit, and substantial elevation gain shouldn't be underestimated. Keep an eye out for mountain goats as you climb the summit along the rubble and snow. Hyndman Peak was incorrectly considered the tallest peak in Idaho until 1934.

Getting There

From Hailey, head northwest on State Hwy 75 N for six miles. Turn right onto East Fork Road and continue for four miles to the town Triumph. Continue past Triumph for another mile until you come to Forest Service Road 203. Make a sharp left turn up the hill and follow it for about 4.5 miles until you reach the trailhead. There are many unmarked side roads on Road 203 which can be confusing. Stay on the main road, and keep left when confronted with turnoffs that look compelling. The route can be rough, but high clearance or 4WD vehicles aren't required. There is a camp toilet at the trailhead.

Route Description

From the parking lot, take the small trail on the east side of the lot toward Hyndman Creek, not the 4x4 road. Almost immediately, you will come upon Hyndman Creek. To circumvent the creek, take the path on the left to a small bridge crossing. For the first few miles, you will gradually climb amongst the aspens alongside the creek, with Cobb Peak dominating the skyline in the distance.

About three miles into the hike (north turn, 8,250ft), the trail becomes steeper as it turns north, heading to the left of Cobb Peak. After gaining about 400 feet in elevation and trading aspen for sagebrush, the trail levels out in a meadow with a small pond. Continue on the trail to the right of the pond, where you will reach another creek crossing. Directly after the creek, you will again find a steep sage-sided trail. As you hike up this incline, gaining almost 600 feet in half a mile, you will hear the creek crashing against the rocks as it pours down a small canyon to the right of the trail. The top of this rise (upper meadows, 9,400ft) will present your first proper view of Hyndman Peak. This is a great place to take a break and capture a quick photo.

The trail soon leaves the tree line as it wanders toward the saddle through Hyndman Basin. About half a mile into this section, or 4.75 miles from the trailhead, you will come across Sundance Lake. Depending on the time of year and snowpack, this may be the last reliable point to fill up on water. Past the lake, the trail begins to rapidly gain elevation as it climbs alongside the creek, gaining 1,000 feet in one mile from Sundance Lake to the top of the saddle.

Hyndman Creek Trail heading toward Cobb Peak.

The route shortly after the creek crossing with Hyndman Peak in the distance.

Sundance Lake in Hyndman Basin.

As the trail deteriorates in the rocky fields, keep an eye out for cairns as you head toward the saddle's right side through boulder-filled terrain. Once at the base of the saddle, which connects Hyndman Peak with Old Hyndman Peak, look for the steep scree trail that will take you to the top. At the top of the saddle (10,780ft), you are introduced to a breathtaking view of Wild Horse Canyon to the northeast and the summit of Hyndman Peak to the northwest.

Follow the trail on the saddle to the left (north) toward the summit. You will gain about 1,200 feet in .6 miles, so be prepared for a strenuous climb. As you move up the saddle and onto the summit block, hugging the right ridge, the trail will disappear periodically, so be prepared to scramble up off-path. It is worth mentioning that you should never be directly on the cliff's edge at any point. The rock is reasonably stable, but always be aware of climbers below you and avoid dropping rocks down the trail.

Author's Note

My first time hiking Hyndman Peak, I began climbing up to the summit before reaching the saddle, thinking I would save time. The rugged terrain slowed me down considerably, resulting in a much longer ascent time. Head up the saddle first before turning toward the summit!

Hyndman Peak from shortly after Sundance Lake.

Hikers on Hyndman Peak's saddle.

Hyndman Basin from the saddle.

The route up Hyndman Peak from the saddle.

The summit provides excellent views of the Pioneer Mountains, including Goat Mountain to the north and Old Hyndman and Cobb Peak to the south. You can see the Lost River Range to the east on a clear day.

Author's Note

I go back and forth between Class 2 and Class 3 on what climbing rating this summit push should be. While it is theoretically possible to climb this without using your hands to progress, most people following the route up will find themselves in situations where they must navigate small ledges using handholds for support. These sections have limited exposure, but they still may be overwhelming for new climbers. Be prepared for this possibility.

The northwest view atop Hyndman Peak.

Hyndman Peak's northeast face.

Elevation Profile

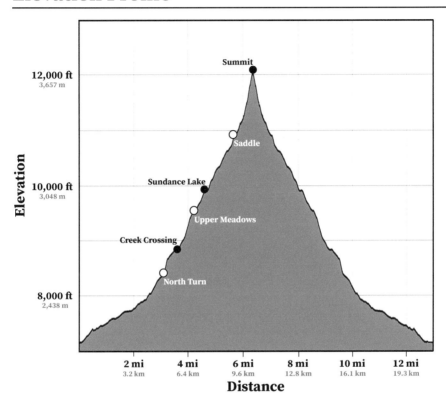

GPS Waypoints

Trailhead - 7,055 ft
N43° 41.975' W114° 11.300'

North Turn - 8,250 ft
N43° 43.253' W114° 08.681'

Creek Crossing - 8,740 ft
N43° 43.621' W114° 08.971'

Upper Meadows - 9,400 ft
N43° 43.947' W114° 08.601'

Sundance Lake - 9,790 ft
N43° 44.257' W114° 08.232'

Saddle - 10,780 ft
N43° 44.696' W114° 07.328'

Summit - 12,009 ft
N43° 44.963' W114° 07.874'

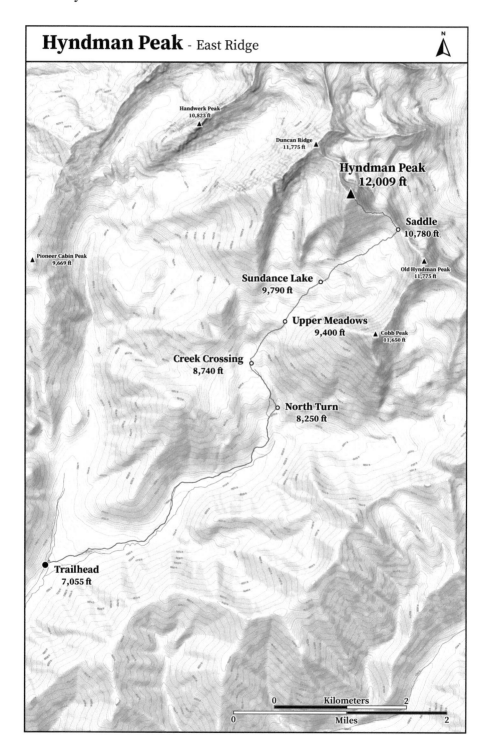

Hyndman Peak - East Ridge

N

Handwerk Peak
10,823 ft

Duncan Ridge
11,775 ft

Hyndman Peak
12,009 ft

Saddle
10,780 ft

Pioneer Cabin Peak
9,669 ft

Old Hyndman Peak
11,775 ft

Sundance Lake
9,790 ft

Upper Meadows
9,400 ft

Cobb Peak
11,650 ft

Creek Crossing
8,740 ft

North Turn
8,250 ft

Trailhead
7,055 ft

0   Kilometers   2

0   Miles   2

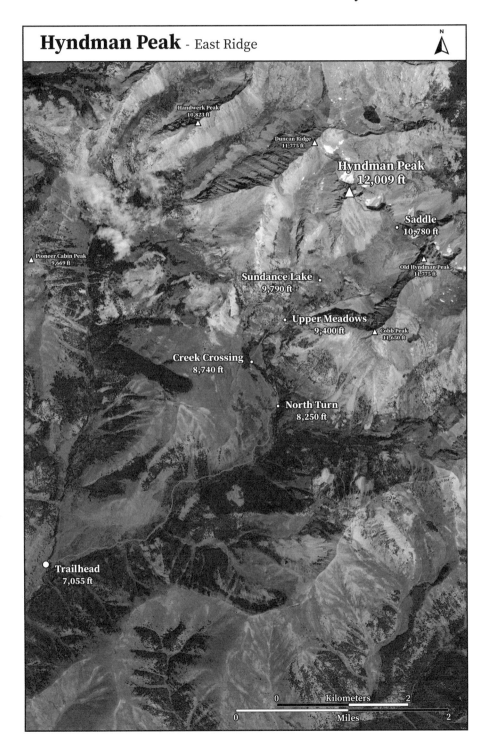

Hyndman Peak - East Ridge

Lost River Range

Rising out of the Big Lost River Valley on the west and the Little Lost River Valley on the east, the Lost River Range runs southeast for 75 miles, starting just south of Challis, Idaho, and ending north of Arco. This Central Idaho range is home to seven of Idaho's Twelvers. In 1983, the largest earthquake in Idaho's history hit the Lost River Range. This 7.3 magnitude earthquake caused the range to gain an average of five feet in elevation, with Borah Peak in particular gaining about a foot and a half in height. Part of the resulting 21-mile-long fault scarp is visible on the drive up to the Borah trailhead. Much of the exposed rock on the range is lithified ocean sediment, so keep an eye out for fossils when hiking these peaks.

Sacajawea Peak and Mount Idaho from Chicken Out Ridge.

Borah Peak from Mount Idaho.

Borah Peak

12,662 feet (3,859 meters)

Highest Twelver

Climbing Route: Southwest Ridge
Rating: Class 3
Elevation Gain: 5,600 feet
Round Trip Distance: 8.2 miles
Round Trip Time: 9.5 hours
Water: There is no consistent water source on this route
Map: USGS: Borah Peak, U.S. Forest Service: Salmon-Challis - Challis (east)

Name: The mountain was named after William Borah, a United States Senator from Idaho
First Ascent: USGS surveyor T.M. Bannon in 1912
Nearest Town: Mackay, ID
Prominence: 5,982 feet (1,823 meters) One of only three peaks in Idaho that are classified as ultra-prominent. Borah is the 27th most prominent peak in the lower 48 states.

Overview

As the highest point in Idaho, Borah Peak towers over the surrounding mountains in the Lost River Range. This classic hike is the most popular Twelver and is home to the aptly named "Chicken Out Ridge," a knife-edged scramble that sees many hikers call it quits. There is a well-defined trail for much of the hike, though the final stretch up the mountain may be difficult to navigate for novice climbers. The Borah Glacier, a rock glacier located on the north slope of the mountain, is the only active glacier in Idaho.

Getting There

From Mackay, head northwest on US-93N for 20.1 miles. Turn right onto Birch Springs Road. The trailhead begins at the end of the road, just over three miles up. The road is well maintained and does not require high clearance or 4WD. The scarp along this road shortly before the trailhead is from the 1983 Borah Peak earthquake. The trailhead has a small campground (small fee to use) and bathrooms. Water is not provided at the campground. Both the campground and parking lot fill up fast during peak climbing season, so if you want a spot be sure to arrive well before the rush of evening climbers.

Route Description

The trail begins just to the right of two Borah Peak plaques on the east end of the parking lot. For the first mile or so, this well-traversed trail moves through shrubs, grasses, and eventually pine trees along a rocky drainage. This early section of the hike has a relatively gradual incline, but don't be fooled; this route is aggressively steep. At around the one-mile mark, the trail makes a left turn to the north toward a small saddle. You will make a right turn east at the top of this saddle (lower saddle, 8,600ft). This is where the incline truly begins. This steep winding trail climbs its way up through fallen trees and exposed roots toward the ridgeline, gaining 1,500 feet in just under a mile. It can be pretty strenuous, so **hiking poles are recommended.**

Gnarled roots and trees shortly after the lower saddle on Borah Peak.

A hiker walking along the ridge toward Chicken Out Ridge.

At the top of the ridge (10,100ft), you are greeted with a dramatic view of Borah. This is an excellent place for a water break as you catch your breath and take in the view. From the top of the ridge, follow the trail southeast for one mile as it moves along the rim toward the uniquely multicolored rock of Chicken Out Ridge (COR). COR may look daunting as you approach it, but don't fret; much of the elevation gain is made on a trail right before the ridge begins, leaving little actual gain during the scramble. Just before the base of COR, the trail increases in steepness as the path becomes filled with loose rock. There may be several intertwining trails during this section, but keep heading up toward the rust-colored spine of the ridge.

Author's Note

One downside of hiking Borah before sunrise is that you may get to Chicken Out Ridge while it is still pitch black out. On a recent trip to the top, I encountered a freezing solo hiker in the dark who was unfamiliar with the terrain and smartly decided not to continue forward onto the ridge without assistance. I helped him across, but not every hiker will have a guide to cross this section. If you are new to scrambling, I recommend getting to Chicken Out Ridge when morning light can illuminate it.

Chicken Out Ridge (COR)

Before beginning COR (11,290ft), I recommend stowing your hiking poles, putting on gloves, and securing any loose items inside your pack. With COR being a repetitive jumble of rock with few distinct features, trying to follow specific instructions may be detrimental to a climber. Instructions here may be misinterpreted and accidentally lead someone off the trail into a dangerous area. With that in mind, the guidance here will be more general.

The ridge is only a quarter of a mile and gains around 450 feet in elevation. The rock on the ridge is generally solid, so carefully move uphill until you hit the crux of the route, a 20-foot downclimb that ends on the snow bridge or, if climbed late in the season, a dry saddle. The strategy for COR is to stay on the ridge's spine for most of the climb. You may find a trail toward the right early in the climb, but eventually, you will need to get back up on the spine before ending at the snow bridge. **DO NOT ATTEMPT TO BYPASS COR WITH A TRAIL TO THE LEFT.** Attempting to bypass the ridge can put hikers in hazardous terrain that has required Search and Rescue evacuations in the past. The top of the crux is often marked with a climbing rope, but don't rely on it for pathfinding, as it may not always be there.

Chicken Out Ridge with the snow bridge visible.

Hikers beginning the first scramble on Chicken Out Ridge.

COR can be a bottleneck during the late
morning. Factor this into your timeline.

Hikers downclimbing on COR.

The crux at the end of COR. Be cautious using any climbing rope not set by your group.

The route from atop the crux with Borah Peak in the distance.

Author's Note

A common mistake I have observed people make is not following the obvious path after descending the crux and crossing the snow bridge. I believe they think Chicken Out Ridge is not over and so they are avoiding what they see as the dangerous left path. Once you get down the crux, take the path! Otherwise you will spend hours climbing a pointless and dangerous ridge.

Once down the crux (11,750ft), cross the small saddle and take the obvious trail to the left toward the summit. This trail eventually leads to the upper saddle (11,760ft), a great place to look over the summit, plan a route and prepare for the final push. This final push ascends 900 feet on very loose rock in under half a mile. While not as notorious as COR, this section is incredibly challenging on the body, especially given the high altitude.

Take one of the two trails that head up toward a rocky scar on the face. The trail may be hard to follow here, so keep an eye out for cairns. As you near the summit, the path becomes steeper and the rock looser. Be careful not to drop any rocks on other hikers below you. After a strenuous climb to the top, you will be greeted with outstanding views of Sacajawea Peak, Mount Idaho, and Leatherman Peak to the south.

The snow bridge past Chicken Out Ridge in early July.

The snow bridge past Chicken Out Ridge in early September.

Author's Note

On this final summit push, I have witnessed people climb off-trail, get over-whelmed, and then give up on summiting less than 100 vertical feet from the top. Stick to the route and you shouldn't ever feel like you might plummet off a cliff. And don't be afraid to take a break. Sometimes a brief rest is all it can take to motivate yourself to continue forward.

Borah Peak from the upper saddle. Notice the two trails toward the beginning of the summit climb.

The route up Borah Peak's summit.

The southeast view from atop Borah Peak.

Hikers heading up toward Borah Peak's summit.

Elevation Profile

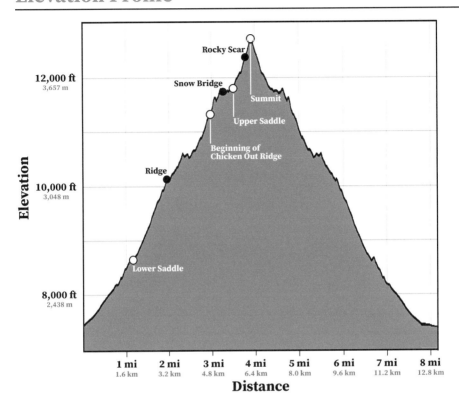

GPS Waypoints

Trailhead - 7,430 ft
N44° 07.953' W113° 50.069'

Lower Saddle - 8,600 ft
N44° 08.245' W113° 49.111'

Ridge - 10,100 ft
N44° 08.130' W113° 48.357'

Beginning of COR - 11,290 ft
N44° 07.742' W113° 47.437'

Snow Bridge - 11,750 ft
N44° 07.739' W113° 47.201'

Upper Saddle - 11,760 ft
N44° 07.893' W113° 47.060'

Rocky Scar - 12,300 ft
N44° 08.121' W113° 46.935'

Summit - 12,662 ft
N44° 08.243' W113° 46.866'

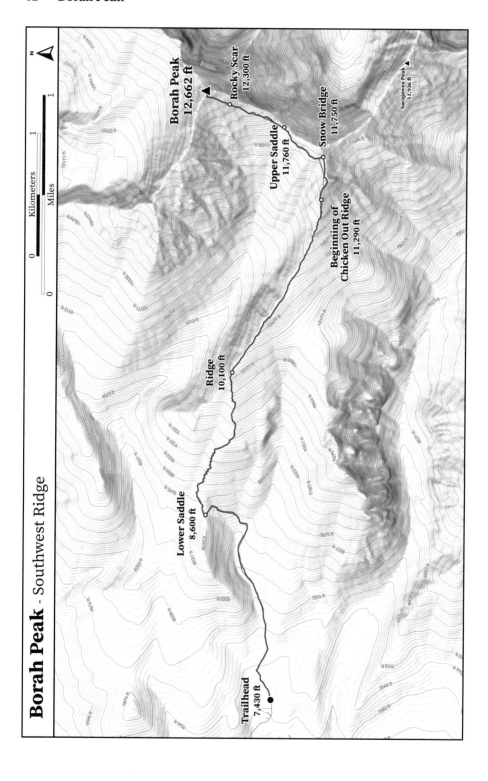

Borah Peak - Southwest Ridge

Borah Peak
12,662 ft

Rocky Scar
12,300 ft

Upper Saddle
11,760 ft

Snow Bridge
11,750 ft

Sacajawea Peak
11,936 ft

Beginning of
Chicken Out Ridge
11,290 ft

Ridge
10,100 ft

Lower Saddle
8,600 ft

Trailhead
7,430 ft

Kilometers

Miles

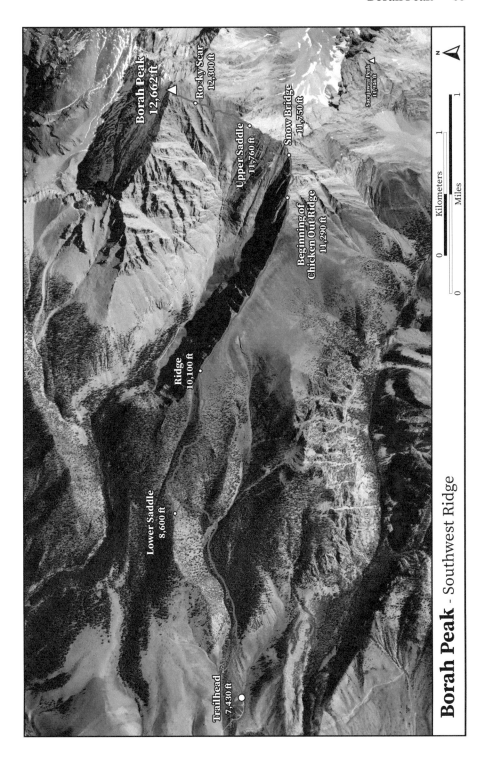

Borah Peak - Southwest Ridge

Mount Idaho from the east.

Mount Idaho

12,065 feet (3,677 meters)

7th Highest Twelver

Climbing Route: West Ridge / Southwest Face
Rating: Class 3
Elevation Gain: 5,150 feet
Round Trip Distance: 7.5 miles
Round Trip Time: 9 hours
Water: Water is accessible for the first two miles from Elkhorn Creek.

Map: USGS Elkhorn Creek, U.S. Forest Service: Salmon-Challis - Challis (east)
Name: Unofficially labeled Mount Idaho. This mountain is also known as Elkhorn Peak
First Ascent: Unkown
Nearest Town: Mackay, ID
Prominence: 1,066 feet (324 meters)

Overview

The rugged Mount Idaho gives climbers a chance to take in all that a Lost River climb offers. Steep talus chutes, sharp ridge scrambles, tortuous forests, and ample route finding eventually reward hikers with incredible views of Borah Peak. **The rock-filled chutes of Mount Idaho are very dangerous! A helmet is strongly recommended, especially when climbing near others.**

Getting There

Besides the Borah Peak Trailhead, this is one of the more accessible Lost River trailheads. From Mackay, head northwest on US-93N for 15.2 miles. Turn right onto Elkhorn Creek Road. Continue up this rough road for just under a mile, keeping the creek to your left. Avoid the left turn about half a mile in that would take you north across the creek to the wrong side. Low-clearance vehicles can make it up fairly high on this road, but high ground clearance is likely needed to make it to the trailhead, which begins at the end of the road.

Route Description

Take the small single-track path heading northeast from the trailhead as it travels above Elkhorn Creek. Within the first half mile, you will cross the creek twice, eventually ending up on its right (southern) side. Shortly after the second creek crossing, the trail becomes steeper, gaining about 500 feet in just over a quarter mile.

The top of this incline (forest, 8,100ft) sees you leaving the sage and grass for thick pine trees and lava rock. For 1.25 miles, you will walk through the trees alongside the creek as it gains 1,150 feet. The trail can be tricky to follow as it moves through the pines, so keep an eye out for rock cairns.

Author's Note

If you lose the trail in the forest, don't stress about it. As long as you are following the creek up to the rock field at 9,250ft you should be fine. Similarly, if you ascend the wrong rock field you should be able to course correct and merge over to the correct field as you climb. Look for the distinct rock towers above you and aim for the right of them.

Pine trees and lava rocks are a common sight on the lower elevation of Mount Idaho.

The route up the rock field toward Mount Idaho's West Ridge. Aim for the right of the distinct rock towers.

At around 8,800 feet, about 1.6 miles into the hike, the trail will cross from the south side of the creek to the north (creek crossing). From this crossing, continue for a quarter mile until you reach the rock field at 9,250 feet. Head north up the rock field for about half a mile. This is a steep scramble that will require quite a bit of route finding. Scramble up the field toward the ridge to the right of a rock tower outcropping. At the top of this ridge (10,600ft), you will get an excellent look at Mount Idaho.

Follow a trail northeast across the talus field toward the saddle. You will come across the first of two rocky spines at the saddle on the West Ridge. This first spine, the longest of the two, is covered in incredibly sharp white rock, so **gloves are highly recommended**. The first half of the spine is a "choose your own path" type climb, though keep an eye out for rock cairns, as they may lead you to an eroded trail on the left (north) about midway up that allows you to bypass much of the sharp rock. Shortly after crossing the spine, you will see the second scramble at the end of a barren flat. Look for a small trail toward the right side of the scramble to help on the ascent.

The route from the ridge to Mount Idaho's summit.

The first scramble to the second scramble.

Upper rest to the rock chute.

The route as viewed from the rock chute.

The top of this second scramble, otherwise known in this book as the upper rest (11,140ft), makes for a great resting spot before beginning the last stretch of the climb. From the upper rest, continue northeast following cairns until you are below the cliffs of Mount Idaho's West Face. Here the path will make a right (east) turn as you make your way below a series of intersecting rocky chutes. The trail ends at a large cairn pile, which signifies the point to turn uphill (bottom of chute).

Author's Note

Of all the standard routes up these mountains, the summit chutes on Mount Idaho have been where I have witnessed the most consistent rockfall. On my last climb, I triggered a massive slide below me. Thankfully I was the only hiker on the mountain, but not everyone will have that dangerous luxury. Please be careful here!

Ascending these steep talus and scree chutes sees you gaining 500 feet in under a quarter mile. There is no one correct way up this final stretch, though generally, you want to stay left of the visible path during this uphill section, as the path is a downhill scree trail. Use the large rocks and cliff walls for traction. The summit is easy to miss in favor of a false summit on the right, so keep left as you near the top. Once on top, you will get a spectacular view of Sacajawea Peak and Borah Peak to the north, Mount Corruption to the east, and White Cap Peak and Leatherman Peak to the south.

The route down the mountain is slightly different than the ascent. You will retrace your steps down the summit, past the upper rest, and across the two scramble sections. Once you reach the saddle talus field at around 10,770 feet, turn left (downhill turn) down the scree into the bowl instead of walking over to the ridge. This option requires a bit of bushwhacking, but it is easier than downclimbing the rockfield you climbed up during the ascent. Descend the steep scree until you enter the forested bowl. From there, head southwest, reconnect with the trail, and follow the regular route back down.

Author's Note

I have seen several trip reports where climbers continued descending down the scree chutes off Mount Idaho's summit into the bowl. Thinking this may be a new "standard" method of descending, I tried it myself. I highly recommend climbers NOT do this. While a specific chute may gradually lead into the bowl, most of them cliff out. The particular GPX trail I followed led me to aggressive Class 4 terrain, where I broke a hiking pole and made questionable downclimbing decisions. Stick to the standard routes for descending listed in this book.

The path up one of Mount Idaho's rock chutes.

Mount Idaho from the southwest basin.

Elevation Profile

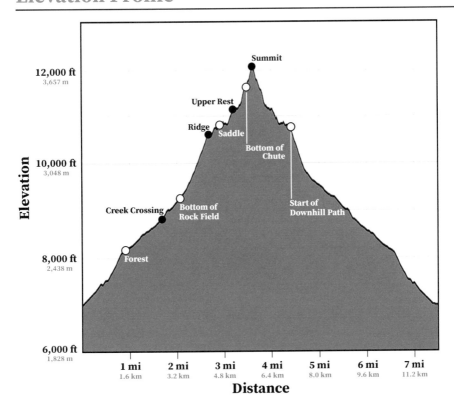

GPS Waypoints

Trailhead - 6,985 ft
N44° 04.513' W113° 49.229'

Forest - 8,100 ft
N44° 04.783' W113° 48.289'

Creek Crossing - 8,810 ft
N44° 05.262' W113° 47.754'

Bottom of Rock Field - 9,250 ft
N44° 05.521' W113° 47.559'

Ridge - 10,600 ft
N44° 05.966' W113° 47.474'

Saddle - 10,780 ft
N44° 06.087' W113° 47.330'

Upper Rest - 11,140 ft
N44° 06.232' W113° 47.001'

Bottom of Chute - 11,580 ft
N44° 06.261' W113° 46.765'

Summit - 12,065 ft
N44° 06.358' W113° 46.668'

Start of Downhill Turn - 10,770 ft
N44° 06.087' W113° 47.330'

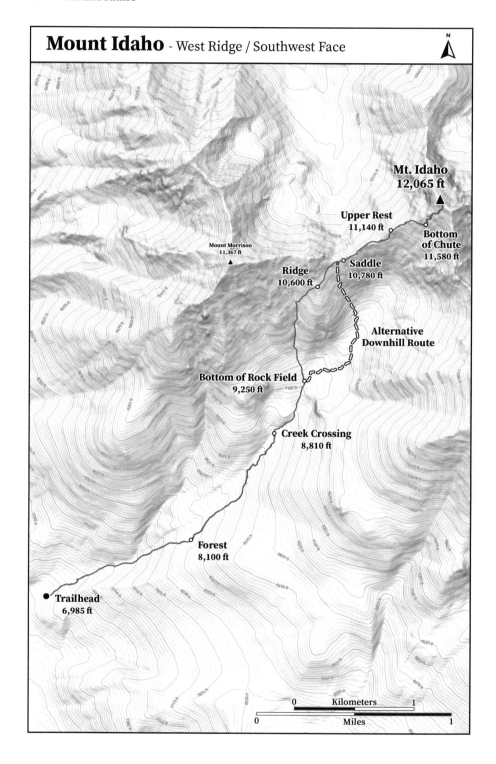

Mount Idaho - West Ridge / Southwest Face

N

Mt. Idaho
12,065 ft
▲

Upper Rest
11,140 ft

Bottom
of Chute
11,580 ft

Mount Morrison
11,367 ft
▲

Ridge
10,600 ft

Saddle
10,780 ft

Alternative
Downhill Route

Bottom of Rock Field
9,250 ft

Creek Crossing
8,810 ft

Forest
8,100 ft

Trailhead
6,985 ft

0   Kilometers   1

0   Miles   1

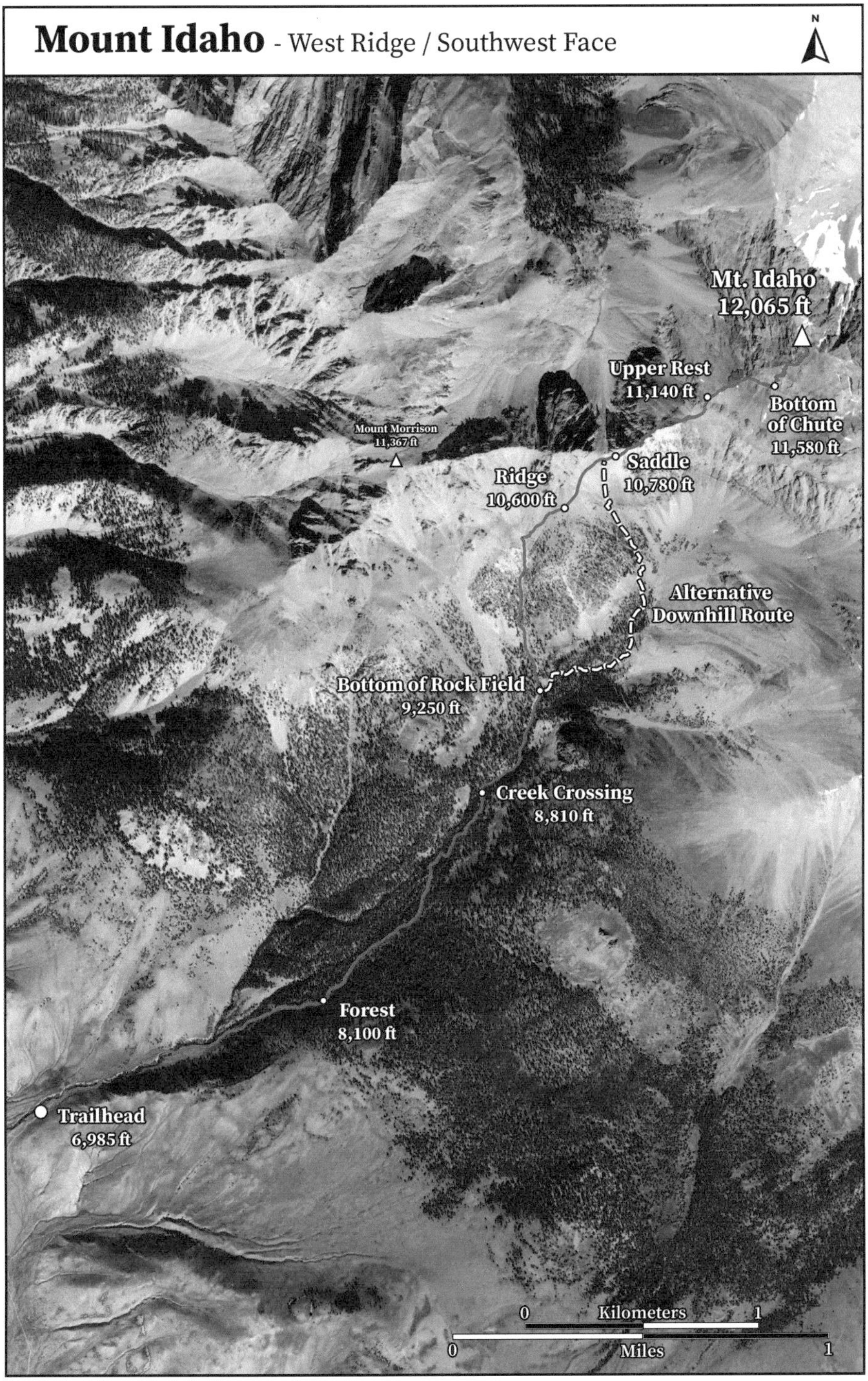

Mount Idaho - West Ridge / Southwest Face

N

Mt. Idaho
12,065 ft

Upper Rest
11,140 ft

Bottom
of Chute
11,580 ft

Mount Morrison
11,367 ft

Ridge
10,600 ft

Saddle
10,780 ft

Alternative
Downhill Route

Bottom of Rock Field
9,250 ft

Creek Crossing
8,810 ft

Forest
8,100 ft

Trailhead
6,985 ft

0   Kilometers   1

0   Miles   1

Leatherman Peak from the north.

Leatherman Peak (East Route)
12,228 feet (3,727 meters)
2nd Highest Twelver

Climbing Route: Northeast Gully
Rating: Class 3
Elevation Gain: 4,000 feet
Round Trip Distance: 8.3 miles
Round Trip Time: 8 hours
Water: Water is easily accessible for the first 2.5 miles from the West Fork Pahsimeroi River
Map: USGS Leatherman Peak, U.S. Forest Service: Salmon-Challis - Challis (east)

Name: Named after Henry Leatherman, a 19th-Century teamster in the Lost River Valley. He is buried within sight of the mountain
First Ascent: T.M. Bannon, a USGS surveyor in 1914
Nearest Town: Mackay, ID
Prominence: 1,667 feet (508 meters)

Author's Note
There are two Leatherman Peak routes listed in this book. I highly recommend this eastern route for beginner and intermediate climbers.

Overview

The eastern approach of Idaho's 2nd tallest mountain takes hikers deep into the stunning and seldom visited Pahsimeroi Valley. This eastern route, now considered the standard route, is challenging to reach in a vehicle compared to the western approach, but it provides a safer route up the mountain through a panoramic setting. The trail is well-defined until the gully. Be prepared for light scrambling just below the summit.

Getting There

From Mackay, head northwest on US-93 N for 21.9 miles. Before the Mount Borah Historical Marker, turn right onto Doublespring Pass Road. Continue on this road for 10.5 miles. Make a sharp right turn onto NF-117, which you will stay on for the next six miles as you move southeast. Continue on this dirt road until it merges onto NF-118/Upper Pahsimeroi Road heading south, which you will stay on until the trailhead.

About one mile after the merge, high clearance and AWD/4WD become necessary for the remainder of the drive due to the presence of constant boulders and ruts in the road. At 4.6 miles into NF-118, you will pass by the historic Zollinger Range Cabin, and just beyond that, an unlocked gate. Shortly after the gate, you will come to a junction with a sign pointing left toward East Fork Upper Pahsimeroi and right toward West Fork Upper Pahsimeroi. Turn right toward the West Fork. The trailhead is at the end of the road, three miles from this turnoff.

Route Description

The trail begins at the southern end of the parking area. Almost immediately, the trail crosses over the creek twice. Shortly after the second crossing, you arrive at a junction with two signs on a tree pointing toward Pass Lake or Merriam Lake. Take the trail heading for Pass Lake. Not far from here, you will come across one last sign, a larger one that reads, "Leatherman Pass Trail" in large font. Again continue on the trail toward Leatherman Pass.

Pahsimeroi Valley from the Northeast Gully.

A creek in the upper meadows on the way to Leatherman Peak.

The first section of this hike sees you gradually climbing alongside the West Fork Pahsimeroi River on an obvious trail, gaining only 1,000 feet in two miles. You will cross over the river a few times on bridges and rocks as you head toward the high meadows. At 9,000 feet, you will enter the high meadows, where you will get your first look at Leatherman Peak and Leatherman Pass. As you continue through the meadows, keep an eye out for the disappearance of the pine trees about a half mile down the trail.

When the trees disappear, that signifies the time to turn left (southeast) off the trail and head for the scree-filled gully up toward Leatherman Peak. More specifically, a lone pine tree on the left side of the trail about 2.5 miles into the hike marks the moment to leave the path (tree turnoff). It is important to leave the trail here, as staying on the trail would take you to Pass Lake instead of Leatherman Peak's summit.

As you approach the gully, look for disturbed rock signifying the route (scree climb). There may be a few interweaving paths during this early stage in the climb, but they should all join together as the track progresses. Make your way up the steep scree alongside a rock wall, which should be on your right for the climb until you plateau in the bowl at 10,700 feet. The bowl is about 1,400 feet above and .8 miles away from the valley.

The route up Leatherman Peak from the tree turnoff.

Mount Idaho and Borah Peak from the Northeast Gully on Leatherman Peak.

Once in the bowl, move south toward the talus slopes. From the bowl to the top of the ridge, you will gain about 1,000 feet in .4 miles. As you approach the steep talus slope, you will notice two trails climbing toward the ridge. Climb the trail on the right for about 1,000 feet until you crest the ridge (11,790ft).

These last 450 vertical feet follow the ridge up to the summit, where you will encounter one mild Class 3 scramble. Once above the scramble, the summit is near. At the summit, you will have excellent views of White Cap Peak to the west, Mount Idaho and Borah Peak to the north, Peak 11,909 and Mount Corruption to the northeast, and Bad Rock Peak and Mount Church to the southeast.

Author's Note
Choosing the correct trail can make a huge difference during the climb from the bowl to the ridge. The leftmost trail has looser scree and is far better on the descent, whereas the one on the right climbs alongside solid rock, making the ascent easier. Choose the rightmost trail for the ascent.

The route from the bowl to the ridge on Leatherman Peak.

Leatherman Peak with the route from the ridge to the summit.

Elevation Profile

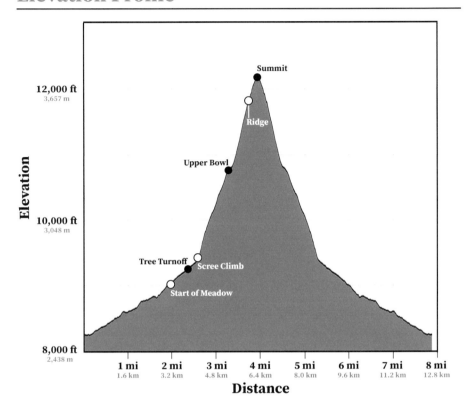

GPS Waypoints

Trailhead - 8,200 ft
N44° 07.750' W113° 43.626'
Start of Meadow - 9,000 ft
N44° 06.260' W113° 44.175'
Tree Turnoff - 9,270 ft
N44° 05.900' W113° 44.255'
Scree Climb - 9,320 ft
N44° 05.840' W113° 44.204'

Upper Bowl - 10,700 ft
N44° 05.337' W113° 43.884'
Ridge - 11,790 ft
N44° 04.994' W113° 43.795'
Summit - 12,228 ft
N44° 04.924' W113° 43.979'

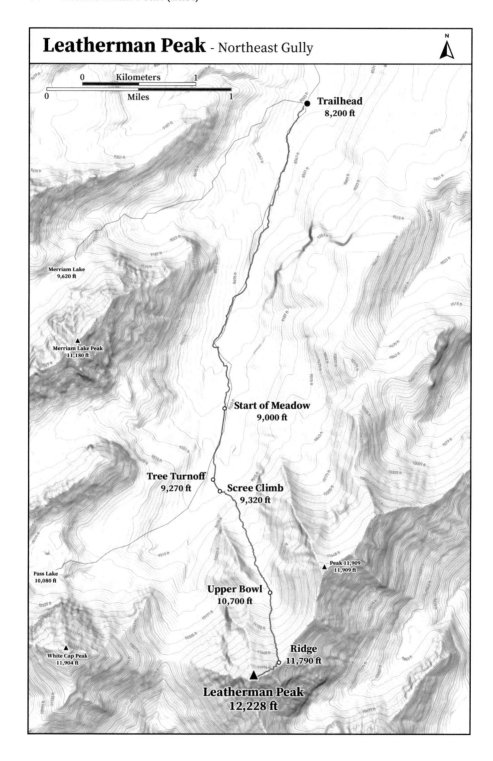

Leatherman Peak - Northeast Gully

N

Kilometers
0   1
Miles
0   1

Trailhead
8,200 ft

Merriam Lake
9,620 ft

▲
Merriam Lake Peak
11,180 ft

Start of Meadow
9,000 ft

Tree Turnoff
9,270 ft

Scree Climb
9,320 ft

Pass Lake
10,080 ft

▲ Peak 11,909
11,909 ft

Upper Bowl
10,700 ft

Ridge
11,790 ft

▲
White Cap Peak
11,904 ft

▲

Leatherman Peak
12,228 ft

Leatherman Peak - Northeast Gully

N

Kilometers
0   1
0   1
Miles

Trailhead
8,200 ft

Merriam Lake
9,620 ft

Merriam Lake Peak
11,180 ft

Start of Meadow
9,000 ft

Tree Turnoff
9,270 ft

Scree Climb
9,320 ft

Peak 11,909
11,909 ft

Pass Lake
10,080 ft

Upper Bowl
10,700 ft

White Cap Peak
11,904 ft

Ridge
11,790 ft

Leatherman Peak
12,228 ft

Leatherman Peak from the southwest.

Leatherman Peak (West Route)
12,228 feet (3,727 meters)
2nd Highest Twelver

Route Name: West Ridge
Rating: Class 3+
Elevation Gain: 3,900 feet
Round Trip Distance: 6.75 miles
Round Trip Time: 8 hours
Water: Water is available from a creek for the first mile, season dependent
Map: USGS Leatherman Peak, U.S. Forest Service: Salmon-Challis - Challis (east)

Name: Named after Henry Leatherman, a 19th-Century teamster in the Lost River Valley. He is buried within sight of the mountain
First Ascent: T.M. Bannon, a USGS surveyor in 1914
Nearest Town: Mackay, ID
Prominence: 1,667 feet (508 meters)

Author's Note

There are two Leatherman Peak routes listed in this book. I only recommend this west route for advanced climbers.

Overview

Once considered the standard route up the mountain, Leatherman's western approach is not for the novice hiker. The rotten talus chutes and treacherous cliffs are difficult to navigate and are better left for the experienced climber. Still, those who do climb the route will find a unique approach and a wonderful view from Leatherman Pass.

Author's Note

It is possible to climb the Northeast Gully using the west approach. Follow the route below until you reach Leatherman Pass. Descend down its northern side until you connect with the Northeast Gully route at the tree turnoff. I don't recommend this option for most people because gaining Leatherman Pass on the ascent and the descent adds over 2,000 feet of elevation gain, putting the total elevation gained at over 6,000 feet. Still, this may be your only option if you do not have a vehicle that can make the eastern drive.

Getting There

From Mackay, head northwest on US-93 N for 12.7 miles. Make a right (northeast) turn onto Sawmill Gulch Road, which is marked with a wooden sign. Stay on this rough road for 2.5 miles until you reach the end. The road can be very steep at the top, so AWD or 4WD is required.

Route Description

From the trailhead (which gains about 2,000 feet in two and a quarter miles as you reach Leatherman Pass), follow the lightly used trail northeast through the pine forest. About half a mile in, the narrow canyon walls widen as you enter the start of the basin. Continue through the basin for another half mile until you reach the end of the tree line below a rock field. Climb up the field, where you will find your first proper view of Leatherman Peak, though Leatherman Pass will remain out of sight, blocked behind a scree field.

From here, continue northeast toward the peak through a scattered forest, where you will connect with the ridge that runs above Lone Cedar Creek. The Pass will come into view as you make your way north up the ridge, where the trail (ridge trail) transitions into a slanted scree field before gaining the Pass.

Leatherman Peak from the southwest basin.

The route from the ridge to Leatherman Pass.

Once on Leatherman Pass (10,500ft), located between White Cap Peak and Leatherman Peak, you will have an excellent view of the West Fork of Pahsimeroi Valley. (If you choose to use the modified west approach up the Northeast Gully, this would be the time to descend down the other side of the Pass.) Take a break and prepare for the upcoming climb, which sees you gaining over 1,700 feet in one mile to reach the summit. From the Pass, head east up the loose scree trail toward Leatherman Peak until the trail fades away at the start of the scramble.

The Leatherman West Ridge is an extended Class 3 scramble where route-finding skills are essential. You will want to stay on the West Ridge as much as possible as you climb up this rotten rock, using chutes and ledges to avoid Class 5 obstacles when necessary. If you are good at route finding, much of this climb is Class 3, though there are a couple of sections where Class 4 is difficult to avoid. Climb slowly and methodically during these sections. When you come to unclimbable rock faces, generally, you will move around them to the left (north) before reconnecting to the ridge. Be very careful of rockfall on this route. If climbing with others, coordinate movements to prevent rockfall exposure.

The route from Leatherman Pass up the West Ridge.

At the summit, you will have excellent views of White Cap Peak to the west, Mount Idaho and Borah Peak to the north, Peak 11,909 and Mount Corruption to the northeast, and Bad Rock Peak and Mount Church to the southeast.

For the descent, you can either carefully retrace your steps down the West Ridge or, if you are okay with adding another two and a half miles to your route, take the Northeast Gully route down to the Pahsimeroi Valley and back up to Leatherman Pass for a safer descent.

Hiker among Leatherman Peak's cliffs.

Author's Note
On my first attempt at climbing the mountain, a friend and I made it above Leatherman Pass and high onto the West Ridge. We were unfamiliar with the route though and quickly found ourselves lost. While looking for the route, I found myself choosing between a small Class 5 cliff and an aggressively steep rock chute. I decided neither was a viable option and moved away from the chute. Seconds after this, a massive rock slide with a few human-sized boulders flew down the chute, right where I would have been climbing. Based on this experience, my friend and I decided the safest option would be to turn around and attempt the peak another day. Never force yourself into dangerous terrain!

A hiker descending Leatherman Peak with White Cap Peak in the distance.

The West Ridge on Leatherman Peak is filled with dangerous cliffs such as these.

Northeast Gully

West Ridge

The Northeast Gully and the West Ridge routes on Leatherman Peak.

Pahsimeroi Valley from Leatherman Peak's West Ridge.

Elevation Profile

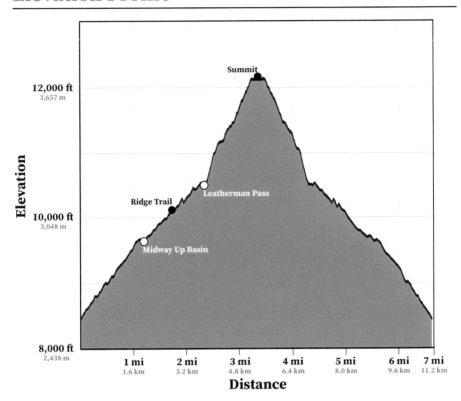

GPS Waypoints

Trailhead - 8,440 ft
N44° 03.867' W113° 46.067'

Midway Up Basin - 9,640 ft
N44° 04.298' W113° 45.073'

Ridge Trail - 10,080 ft
N44° 04.607' W113° 44.796'

Leatherman Pass - 10,500 ft
N44° 05.011' W113° 44.590'

Summit - 12,228 ft
N44° 04.924' W113° 43.979'

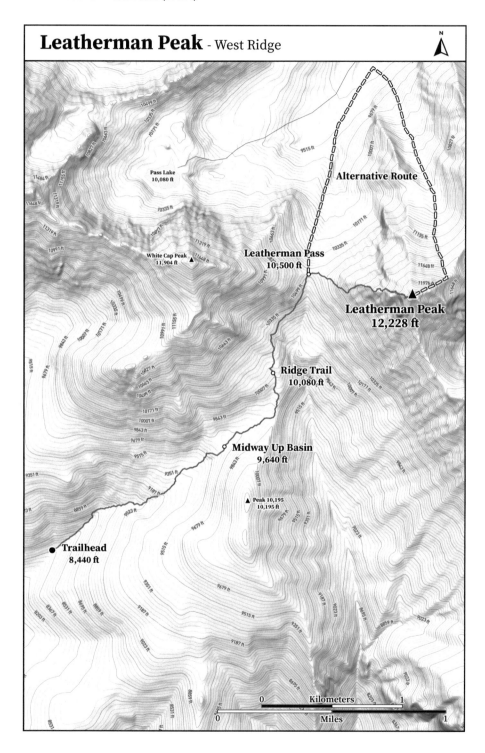

Leatherman Peak - West Ridge

N

Pass Lake
10,080 ft

Alternative Route

White Cap Peak
11,904 ft

Leatherman Pass
10,500 ft

Leatherman Peak
12,228 ft

Ridge Trail
10,080 ft

Midway Up Basin
9,640 ft

Peak 10,195
10,195 ft

Trailhead
8,440 ft

0   Kilometers   1

0   Miles   1

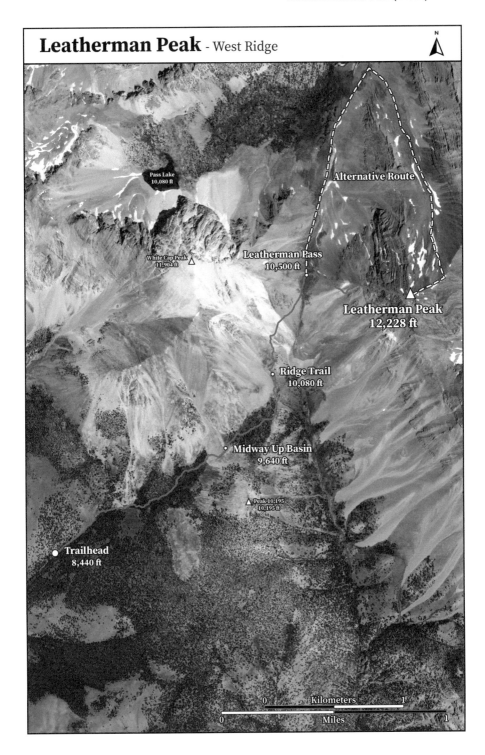

Leatherman Peak - West Ridge

N

Pass Lake
10,080 ft

Alternative Route

White Cap Peak
11,904 ft

Leatherman Pass
10,500 ft

Leatherman Peak
12,228 ft

Ridge Trail
10,080 ft

Midway Up Basin
9,640 ft

Peak 10,195
10,195 ft

Trailhead
8,440 ft

0   Kilometers   1

0   Miles   1

Mount Church from the east.

Mount Church

12,200 feet (3,719 meters)

3rd Highest Twelver

Donaldson Peak

12,023 feet (3,665 meters)

8th Highest Twelver

Climbing Route: North Fork of Jones Creek (Mount Church - East Ridge; Donaldson Peak - West Ridge)

Rating: Class 3

Elevation Gain: 5,400 feet for both (4,650 feet for Donaldson Peak, and an additional 750 feet for Mount Church)

Round Trip Distance: 8.1 miles for both

Round Trip Time: 10 hours for both

Water: Water is available from the creek for the first two miles, and also available from the Upper and Lower Ponds, though these ponds may be dried up by late season

Map: USGS Leatherman Peak, U.S. Forest Service: Salmon-Challis - Challis (east)

Name: Mount Church: No official name. Unofficially named after Idaho Senator Frank Church Donaldson Peak: No official name. Unofficially named after Idaho Supreme Court Justice Charles Donaldson

First Ascent: Unknown for either

Nearest Town: Mackay, ID

Prominence: Mount Church: 919 feet (280 meters) Donaldson Peak: 302 feet (92 meters)

Author's Note

My first time climbing these mountains, I found myself foolishly climbing up the wrong section of the headwall among Class 4 cliffs. On a different climb, a friend injured their hand while we were descending on snow above the upper pond. I recommend people save this climb until they have ample climbing experience to navigate this terrain calmly.

Overview

Mount Church and Donaldson Peak are unique among the Twelvers as they are typically climbed together during the same hike. The hike begins in a rocky creek with a moderately defined trail, but eventually leads you to a high pond in a panoramic cirque that can often appear like a small glacial lake. The long ridge walk between the two mountains, which has several instances of exposed Class 3 climbing, requires spending an extended period of time at altitude, so be sure to watch the skies for any developing thunderclouds.

Donaldson Peak from the southwest.

Getting There

From Mackay, head northwest on US-93N for 10.6 miles. Turn right (northeast) onto Lone Cedar Creek Road, which is marked with a wooden sign. Continue on this road for 1.5 miles until you reach a junction near a ranch. Turn right (south) at the junction and follow the dirt road for 1.6 miles until it reaches the trailhead.

Route Description

From the trailhead, take the small dirt path on the north end of the parking area. This early section of the climb follows the North Fork of Jones Creek as it gains almost 2,400 feet in just over two miles. Shortly into the hike, you will leave the fields and enter the cliffed walls of the creek, where you will pass above an old collapsed cabin. The trail stays high above the creek on the right (east) side before descending into the creek proper.

Stay with the trail as it moves up the drainage through rocks, roots, and shrubs. The trail here is generally easy to follow, but keep an eye out for cairns whenever it crosses the creek. The knuckle-shaped mountain looming in front of you during this stretch is Mount Church. About one mile in, the trail funnels into a narrow canyon with steep rock walls. Here, the thick foliage often obscures the trail, which can be hard to follow as it crosses over to the creek's right (east) side. After the canyon walls open back up, you generally stay on the creek's left (west) side.

Donaldson Peak (left) and Mount Church (right) from the east.

The trail to Mount Church and Donaldson Peak can be tough to follow as it enters the cliffs.

As the trees begin to thin out and large talus fields appear to your left (north), Donaldson Peak will come into view, dominating the sky. The turn to begin climbing up the talus is about a quarter mile from the start of the first talus field. Keep moving along the creek even as the trail disappears until you get to 9,700 feet. Here, you will turn northeast and begin the talus climb up for the upper pond, gaining about 1,100 feet in over half a mile. Head up the rock field, aiming for the left of Donaldson Peak. If you can find the trail about 500 feet up, it will make the trek more straightforward, but if not, keep heading northeast until you reach the plateau at the lower pond (10,620ft).

The route from the creek to the lower pond with Donaldson Peak in the distance.

From the lower pond, head north a short distance toward a crumbling scramble next to the cliffs. Climb up this rugged drain to the cirque between Church and Donaldson, where you will find the upper pond (10,890ft).

The scramble is just shortly past the lower pond and sits below Mount Church and Donaldson Peak.

Directly northeast across the pond is the headwall, where you should see disturbed scree signifying the trail, assuming there isn't any snow. You will gain 800 feet in a little over a quarter mile from the upper pond to the saddle on aggressively steep rotten rock, so **a helmet, poles, and gloves are strongly recommended.**

Author's Note

The difficulty of the hike increases substantially once past the upper pond. Gaining the saddle involves ascending loose talus and scree in terrain that sees you sliding near cliff edges. Once on top of the saddle, the ridge climb to Mount Church is slow going and often puts you in exposed terrain where you must downclimb cliffs on crumbling rock. This all adds up to a slow-going pace high on exposed cliffs. Make sure lightning is not a threat before attempting Mount Church from the saddle, and that your body can handle the extended duration at altitude that is required for this ridge-climb.

A hiker resting at the upper pond below Mount Church.

The headwall to Mount Church / Donaldson Peak's saddle is northeast across the upper pond.

Turn right once you reach the distinct white markings.

Navigate around the pond and climb up directly toward the headwall until you can touch the wall itself. Here you should see distinct white markings on the rock. At this point, there will be a narrow ramp of dirt and scree to your right (southeast). Traverse across and up the steep scree until you come to a large rock formation. Turn left (north) and climb up the rotten rock toward the saddle. Hug the cliff wall to your right if needed, using rock cairns for guidance. You will enter the saddle to the right of a tower near a small rock arch.

Ascend the ramp east of the headwall.

Once you reach the large rock formation, head north toward the saddle.

From the saddle, you can either turn left (north) and climb Mount Church, or turn right (southeast) and climb Donaldson Peak. Donaldson Peak is typically climbed before heading toward Mount Church.

For Donaldson Peak: Once at the saddle (11,710ft), make an immediate right (southeast) turn up toward Donaldson Peak. The summit is very close to the saddle, less than a couple hundred yards away with only 300 feet of gain. Either follow the trail or hug the rocky shelf until you reach the top. The peak is on the left. You will have an outstanding view of Mount Church to the west and No Regrets Peak and Mount Breitenbach to the east.

For Mount Church: At the saddle, turn left (northwest) along the ridge as it climbs up and down on its way to the false peak. The actual summit of Mount Church is .65 miles from the saddle and requires over 500 feet of elevation gain. Route finding will be necessary for much of this section as the trail appears and disappears among the cliffs. You generally want to stay on the ridge as much as possible. There will be a few sections where Class 3 downclimbing to the left will be required, though be careful not to descend too far downhill. Try and get back up onto the ridge whenever possible. The downclimbing sections occur at .2, .35, and .6 miles into the climb, though depending on individual hiker preferences and GPS settings, your results may vary.

Once you reach the false summit (12,000ft), Mount Church's actual top finally appears and is only a short distance, and one downclimb, away. At the top, you will have a striking view of Bad Rock Peak and Leatherman Peak to the north and Donaldson Peak to the south.

Donaldson Peak with the overall route displayed.

The route along the ridge toward Mount Church.

The ridge scramble between Mount Church and Donaldson Peak requires route finding. Be especially careful during the downclimbs.

The upper pond from Mount Church.

Cliff walls shortly into the hike up the North Fork of Jones Creek.

Donaldson Peak from Mount Breitenbach.

Elevation Profile

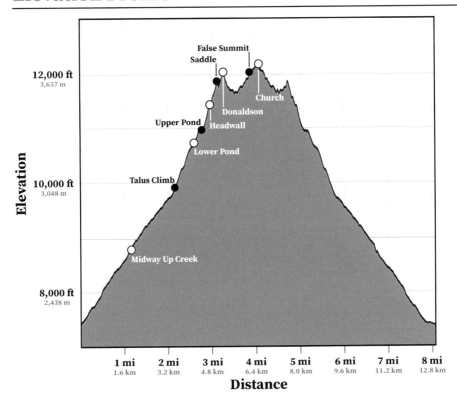

GPS Waypoints

Trailhead - 7,360 ft
N44° 02.064' W113° 43.956'

Midway Up Creek - 8,745 ft
N44° 02.909' W113° 43.563'

Talus Climb - 9,700 ft
N44° 03.361' W113° 42.845'

Lower Pond - 10,620 ft
N44° 03.665' W113° 42.482'

Upper Pond - 10,890 ft
N44° 03.751' W113° 42.449'

Headwall - 11,345 ft
N44° 03.818' W113° 42.233'

Saddle - 11,710 ft
N44° 03.884' W113° 42.108'

Summit of Donaldson Peak - 12,023 ft
N44° 03.842' W113° 42.027'

False Summit - 12,000 ft
N44° 03.968' W113° 42.664'

Summit of Mount Church - 12,200 ft
N44° 03.961' W113° 42.810'

Mt. Church / Donaldson Peak - East/West Ridge

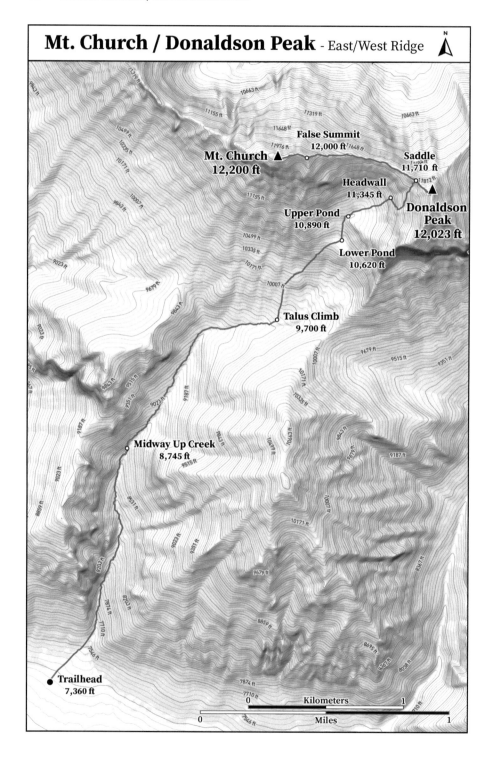

Mt. Church ▲
12,200 ft

False Summit
12,000 ft

Saddle
11,710 ft

Headwall
11,345 ft

Donaldson Peak ▲
12,023 ft

Upper Pond
10,890 ft

Lower Pond
10,620 ft

Talus Climb
9,700 ft

Midway Up Creek
8,745 ft

Trailhead
7,360 ft

Kilometers

Miles

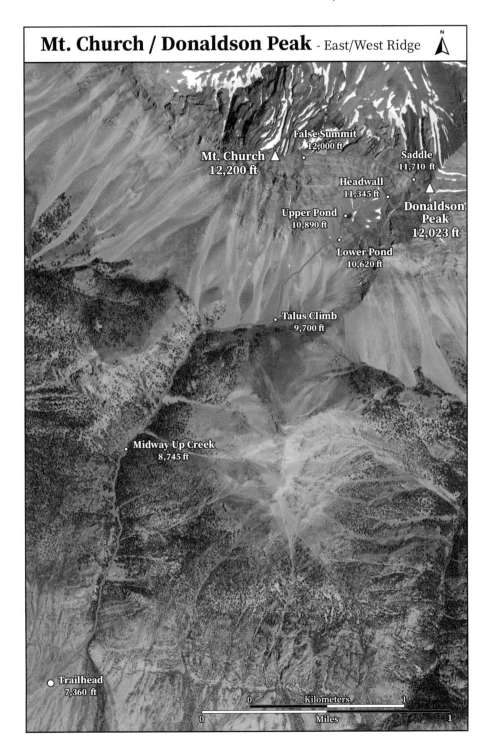

Mt. Church / Donaldson Peak - East/West Ridge

N

False Summit
12,000 ft

Mt. Church ▲
12,200 ft

Saddle
11,710 ft

Headwall
11,345 ft

Donaldson
Peak
12,023 ft ▲

Upper Pond
10,890 ft

Lower Pond
10,620 ft

Talus Climb
9,700 ft

Midway Up Creek
8,745 ft

Trailhead
7,360 ft

Kilometers
0   1

Miles
0   1

Mount Breitenbach from the southeast.

Mount Breitenbach

12,140 feet (3,700 meters)

5th Highest Twelver

Climbing Route: South Ridge
Rating: Class 3
Elevation Gain: 4,600 feet
Round Trip Distance: 7 miles
Round Trip Time: 8.5 hours
Water: Water can be found sporadically in the creek for the first two miles
Map: USGS Leatherman Peak, U.S. Forest Service: Salmon-Challis - Challis (east)

Name: Named after Jake Breitenbach, an Idaho climber that was killed on the 1963 American expedition to Mount Everest by a collapsing ice wall
First Ascent: Unknown. Possibly Wayne Boyer, a notable Idaho climber
Nearest Town: Mackay, ID
Prominence: 620 feet (188 meters)

Overview

The approach hike through Pete Creek can be frustratingly slow, but generally the route up Breitenbach is one of the easier Twelver hikes. The summit isn't visible during the hike until almost near the top, which makes it even more rewarding. The route passes by a small waterfall as well as a fossil-infused scramble. Keep an eye out for bighorn sheep as you near the top.

Getting There

From Mackay, head northwest on US-93N for 8.1 miles. Turn right onto an unnamed dirt road. Continue for 2.1 miles, where you will make a slight left, followed by a slight right. In half a mile, turn right (east) on road 866. In 0.7 miles, turn right (south) onto 866A. In 0.3 miles, keep left at the fork. About 0.3 miles from there, turn left (north). The trailhead will be at the end of the road in one mile. The road can be rough as you near the trailhead, so high clearance is recommended. (Option: If you continue on 866 instead of turning on 866A, you will end up at the old trailhead, which has easier access but adds in a rough creek crossing into the hike)

Route Description

From the trailhead, look for a narrow path heading north alongside and descending into Pete Creek. This small trail ends in the dry creek bed, where for the next mile and a half, it becomes increasingly hard to follow as you gain around 1,600 feet reaching the end of the creek. Follow the cairns and trail when possible, but often, and especially when it is dark, you may have to bushwack up the creek bed toward the mountain. Eventually, the trees and bushes along the creek thin out, and the landscape transforms into wildflowers and thistles, flanked on either side by steep talus. The creek will come to an end shortly after entering this rocky basin.

The trail to Mount Breitenbach through Pete Creek.

The trail shortly into Mount Breitenbach's scree climb.

   From the end of the creek (start of scree), head north up the rock field, with the ultimate goal being to reach the saddle at the end of the bowl. During this section of the hike, you will gain about 2,000 feet of elevation in just under a mile, so be prepared for a steep incline. The trail in this lower portion of the rock field is slim to none, so keep an eye out for rock cairns as you ascend the drainage alongside several unique rock towers. Look for a rocky outcropping midway up the bowl just past a small waterfall at around 10,500 feet.

   From the base of this outcropping (scramble), turn right and carefully climb up the rotten, fossil-embedded rock. At the top of this small scramble, proceed toward the saddle southeast of the false summit, following a faint trail when possible.

A waterfall on Mount Breitenbach just south of the scramble.

The start of the scramble.

Fossils such as this one can be found once entering
the scree field on Mount Breitenbach.

The climb up to the saddle is steep and filled with loose rock, but at the top (11,300ft), you are presented with your first proper view of Breitenbach's summit. This is a great place to take a water break and snap photos of Breitenbach's southeast face. Turn left (northwest) from the saddle and head up the small trail toward the false summit. This is the last major elevation push on the climb, gaining about 600 feet in a quarter mile. At the top (11,900ft), you are now given a fantastic view of the summit and the ridge walk.

> **Author's Note**
> It may be tempting to skip the saddle and climb directly to the false summit, but this would be a mistake. The trail from the saddle provides much better footing and will save you time.

The route up Mount Breitenbach as viewed from Lost River Peak.

Carefully walk the narrow ridge up and down for about half a mile toward the summit. A couple of sections may require handholds along the knife-edged ridge. After one last small incline push, you will be at the summit, where you will be greeted with outstanding views of No Regrets Peak and Donaldson Peak to the north and Lost River Peak to the south.

Author's Note
During my first time descending the mountain, I joined up with another group near the summit who were hoping to follow the saddle over to Lost River Peak, making the trip a double summit. Their logic was sound; we would skip the terrible uphill climb up the Super Gully and instead quickly descend it. However, the group and I failed to realize how difficult the cliffs connecting the two peaks would be to navigate. After debating whether to attempt a small Class 5 move, all parties involved decided to descend Breitenbach instead and climb Lost River Peak another day. Avoid shortcuts unless you are fully prepared and informed about what they will entail!

The ridgewalk as viewed from Mount Breitenbach's summit.

Mount Breitenbach from the saddle.

Elevation Profile

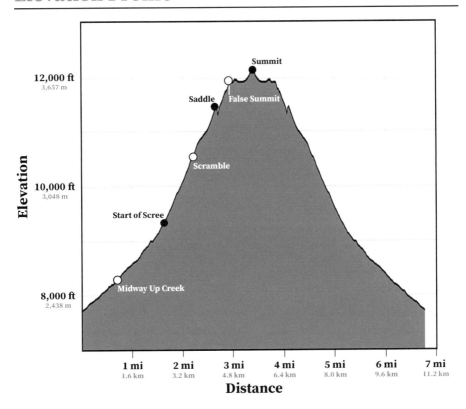

GPS Waypoints

Trailhead - 7,710 ft
N44° 01.456' W113° 40.874'

Midway Up Creek - 8,330 ft
N44° 02.053' W113° 40.695'

Start of Scree - 9,340 ft
N44° 02.659' W113° 40.288'

Scramble - 10,530 ft
N44° 03.093' W113° 40.379'

Saddle - 11,300 ft
N44° 03.434' W113° 40.121'

False Summit - 11,900 ft
N44° 03.517' W113° 40.345'

Summit - 12,140 ft
N44° 03.901' W113° 40.369'

Mount Breitenbach - South Ridge

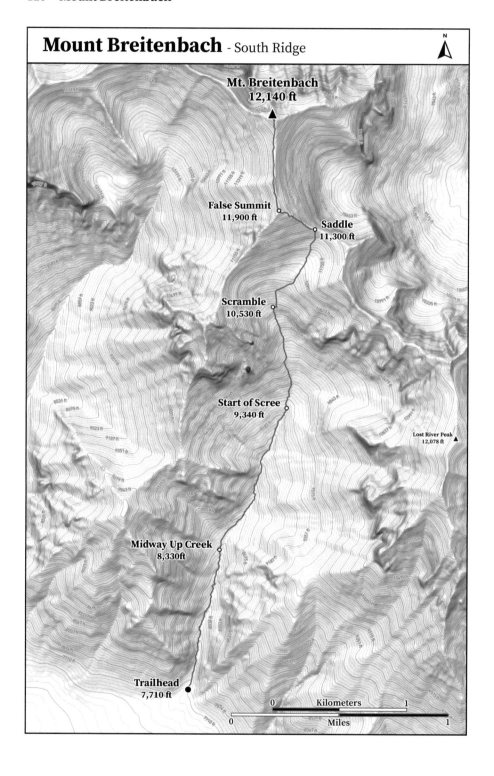

N

Mt. Breitenbach
12,140 ft

False Summit
11,900 ft

Saddle
11,300 ft

Scramble
10,530 ft

Start of Scree
9,340 ft

Lost River Peak
12,078 ft

Midway Up Creek
8,330ft

Trailhead
7,710 ft

Kilometers
0   1

Miles
0   1

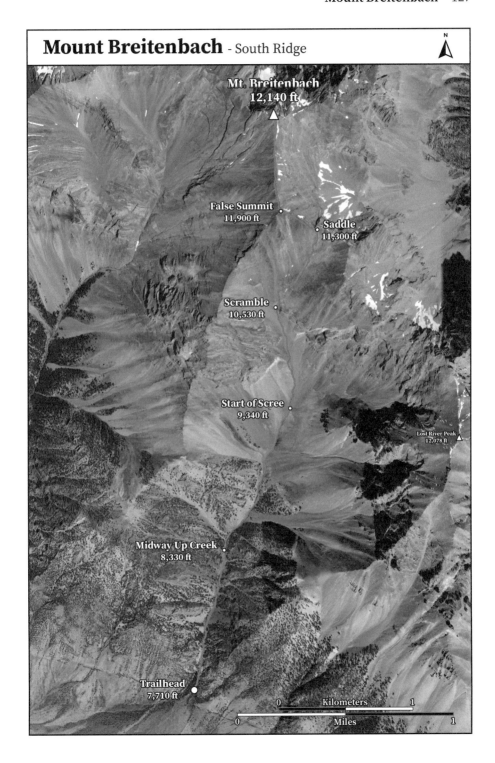

Mount Breitenbach - South Ridge

N

Mt. Breitenbach
12,140 ft

False Summit
11,900 ft

Saddle
11,300 ft

Scramble
10,530 ft

Start of Scree
9,340 ft

Lost River Peak
12,078 ft

Midway Up Creek
8,330 ft

Trailhead
7,710 ft

0   Kilometers   1

0   Miles   1

Lost River Peak from the south.

Lost River Peak
12,078 feet (3,681 meters)
6th Highest Twelver

Climbing Route: Southwest "Super Gully"
Rating: Class 3
Elevation Gain: 4,450 feet
Round Trip Distance: 4.5 miles
Round Trip Time: 7 hours
Water: Despite hiking up alongside a creek, it is typically dry, so plan on packing in your own water

Map: USGS Leatherman Peak, U.S. Forest Service: Salmon-Challis - Challis (east)
Name: No official name. Lost River Peak is the most common name for the mountain
First Ascent: Unknown
Nearest Town: Mackay, ID
Prominence: 678 feet (206 meters)

Overview

The southernmost Twelver in the Lost River Range is home to the unbelievably steep scree-filled "Super Gully." This hike may be short, but it is incredibly mentally and physically exhausting. **A helmet is a must.** Lost River Peak is becoming increasingly popular to hike in the late spring to allow for walking on snow instead of scree. If you climb during the early season, be aware of avalanche conditions.

Getting There

Main Route

From Mackay, head northwest on US-93N for 5.8 miles. Turn right onto Upper Cedar Creek Road. Head northeast on this road for 3.2 miles. Turn left onto the dirt road and take the uphill road heading north. The trailhead is at the end of this road in about one mile. Use the alternate route if the Upper Cedar Creek Road gate is locked.

Alternate Route

From Mackay, head northwest on US-93N for 6.6 miles, or 0.8 miles northwest of Upper Cedar Creek Road. Turn right onto an unmarked dirt road, then make an immediate right. Follow this road for 2.3 miles, where you will keep left at the fork. About 0.6 miles from there, the road turns to the east. Another half mile after that, make a left turn northward. The trailhead is at the end of this road in one mile. The road does not require AWD/4WD, though high clearance is recommended.

Route Description

From the parking area, head east/northeast through low trees and brush as you reach the ridge above the right (south) side of the creek. Head up the slope, staying alongside the ridge above the creek until the trail becomes visible. Shortly after finding the trail, it will turn left and cross down to the creek's north side (creek crossing). This is where the relentless incline begins.

The trail heading through the forest on Lost River Peak.

When you get past this last tree along the trail, make a left toward Lost River Peak's Super Gully.

Make your way up the trail as it climbs 1,200 feet in over half a mile through the forest to the end of the tree line. Deadfall often blocks the path, so be prepared to climb over or navigate around it. Once you reach the very last tree, which stands on its own away from others, you can view the entirety of the route up the Super Gully. This is a great location to catch a breath and put on your helmet before entering the seemingly endless scree field that is the Super Gully.

Author's Note

During my first ascent of this mountain, my friend and I lost the trail shortly after the creek crossing, resulting in us wandering off-trail for a large portion of the climb. While route finding and climbing off-trail are important skills to have, it never hurts to slow down while on the trail so that you don't lose it in the first place. This is especially true when climbing in the dark.

The route up the Super Gully on Lost River Peak.

Super Gully

The Super Gully is a rather infamous landmark in the Idaho Twelver lineup, and is just behind Chicken Out Ridge for notoriety. This southwest-facing gully gains over 1,700 feet in less than three-quarters of a mile on nightmarishly steep scree, which often sees climbers sliding downhill with each step toward the summit. Loose boulders disturbed by hikers repeatedly pummel down this shooting gallery onto the trail below, which is why it is often climbed on snow in the spring. **Hiking poles and a helmet are a must for this route!**

The gully is a massive rock fall hazard. Be mindful of hikers below you and coordinate movements to minimize exposure to rockfall. Follow the trail to the left and climb the gully as it heads toward the narrow cliffed-in bottleneck. The path usually provides solid footing for the lower sections of the gully, but as it enters the cliff walls, the rock becomes looser and makes staying on the trail difficult. Past the bottleneck, the cliff walls will open up, and the trail itself may be too steep to climb from here onward. To avoid sliding downhill with every step, stay to the left of the trail on the larger rocks. This upper section of the gully is the most mentally demanding of the route, but power through it one step at a time.

Once you reach the top of the Super Gully, you can finally see the true summit a quarter mile away. The remainder of the hike is a classic ridge walk. Watch your footing as both sides lead to aggressive falls. You can see the scree bowl route up to Breitenbach to the left of the ridge.

The Lost River Peak ridgewalk with Mount Breitenbach in the distance.

At the summit, you will have great views of Mount Breitenbach to the northwest and Paragon Peak to the southeast. On the descent, the Super Gully trails that proved too steep on the ascent provide excellent opportunities to "scree glissade," allowing you to descend rapidly. Just remember to be conscious of hikers below you.

Looking down the Super Gully on Lost River Peak.

Elevation Profile

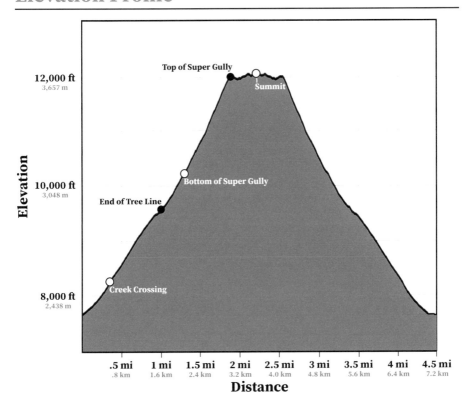

GPS Waypoints

Trailhead - 7,650 ft
N44° 01.069' W113° 40.470'
Creek Crossing - 8,280 ft
N44° 01.203' W113° 40.154'
End of Tree Line - 9,540 ft
N44° 01.615' W113° 39.763'

Bottom of Super Gully - 10,220 ft
N44° 01.844' W113° 39.602'
Top of Super Gully - 11,970 ft
N44° 02.298' W113° 39.373'
Summit - 12,078 ft
N44° 02.526' W113° 39.279'

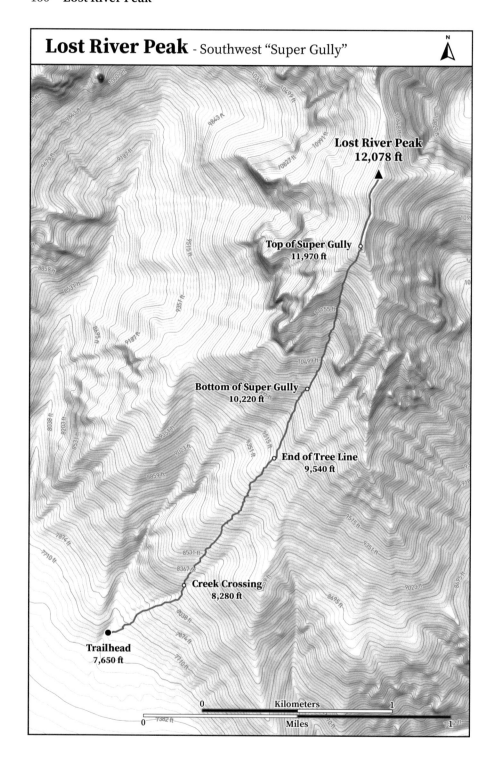

Lost River Peak - Southwest "Super Gully"

N

Lost River Peak
12,078 ft

Top of Super Gully
11,970 ft

Bottom of Super Gully
10,220 ft

End of Tree Line
9,540 ft

Creek Crossing
8,280 ft

Trailhead
7,650 ft

Kilometers
0   1

Miles
0   1

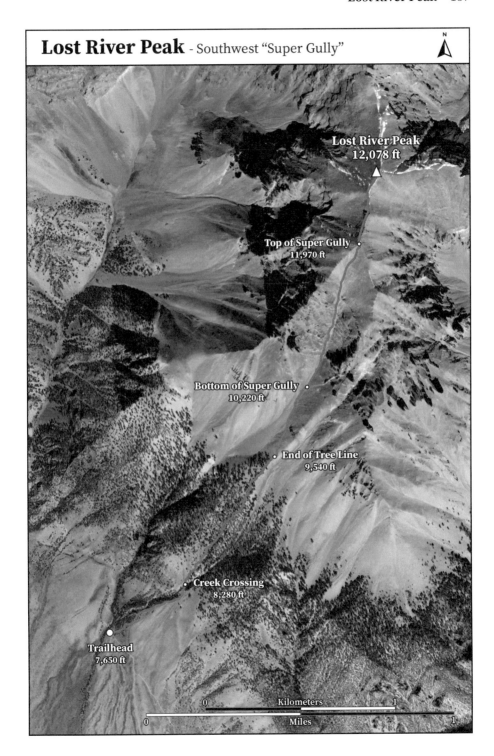

Lost River Peak - Southwest "Super Gully"

N

Lost River Peak
12,078 ft

Top of Super Gully
11,970 ft

Bottom of Super Gully
10,220 ft

End of Tree Line
9,540 ft

Creek Crossing
8,280 ft

Trailhead
7,650 ft

Kilometers

0   1

0   1

Miles

Lemhi Range

The Lemhi Range, located in Eastern Idaho, runs southeast for 100 miles from Salmon until ending in the Snake River Plain. The range lies east and runs parallel to the Lost River Range. This remote and untamed collection of mountains is home to only one of Idaho's Twelvers, though there are many other striking mountains, notably the dome-shaped Bell Mountain. As with the Lost River Range, keep an eye out for fossils while climbing these peaks. Lemhi comes from Limhi, a name used in the Book of Mormon.

Bell Peak from the southeast.

Diamond Peak from the southeast.

Diamond Peak

12,197 feet (3,718 meters)

4th Highest Twelver

Climbing Route: East Ridge
Rating: Class 3
Elevation Gain: 4,150 ft
Round Trip Distance: 5.8 miles
Round Trip Time: 8 hours
Water: No water on route
Map: USGS Diamond Peak, U.S. Forest Service: Caribou-Targee - Dubois, U.S. Forest Service: Salmon-Challis - Challis (east)

Name: Named after its pyramidal shape
First Ascent: T.M. Bannon in 1912
Nearest Town: Terreton, ID (gas only) and Arco, ID
Prominence: 5,377 feet (1,638 meters) One of only three peaks in Idaho that are classified as ultra-prominent

Overview

The tallest mountain in Idaho located outside of the Lost River Range, Diamond Peak rises like a pyramid above the surrounding mountains. The first half of the hike is straightforward on a moderate trail, but once on the ridge the route provides plenty of climbing options for the eager scrambler, though it may overwhelm novice hikers.

Getting There

The drive to the trailhead requires a high-clearance vehicle. From the ID-28N / ID-22E junction, head northwest on ID-28N for 15.8 miles. Turn left onto Pass Creek Road. At 1.8 miles in, turn right to cross over Pass Creek and climb up the hill. Follow this well-worn dirt road as it heads north and passes through a gate half a mile in. One mile past that gate, keep left at the fork and continue west up the road for another 2.5 miles, where you will pass through another gate onto road 240. From this gate onward, the route can be a bit confusing. Reset your odometer and make the following turns:

▶ Make a left turn at 0.5 miles onto road 835. The road requires high clearance and AWD/4WD from here.

▶ Keep left at 0.6 miles.

▶ Make a slight right at 1 mile.

▶ Turn right at 1.8 miles onto road 796.

▶ The trailhead is at 2.4 miles.

Route Description

The route begins with a sign, "End of RTE." If you have a vehicle that can continue on the road past the sign, you will save about half a mile in distance and 500 feet in elevation gain. From the sign, head west on the steep 4x4 road for about a half mile until it transitions into a single-track dirt trail. Stay on this trail as it passes through a rocky scar and eventually into the forest. Continue through the intermittent trees for about half a mile until you hit the saddle below the ridge (9,370ft).

From the saddle, turn right and head through the low pine trees toward the ridge. This rapid climb gains 1,000 feet in half a mile on loose dirt and scree. **Trekking poles are strongly recommended**. Once at the top of the ridge (10,385ft), you will get an excellent view of Diamond Peak and The Riddler to the southwest. While Diamond Peak is in sight, much of the upper route to the summit is not, as the trail generally sticks to the ridge's north.

The trail shortly before the saddle with Diamond Peak in the distance.

The route up Diamond Peak from the ridge toward the scramble.

Follow the ragged trail north and then west for half a mile as it wraps its way toward the peak, gaining around 600 feet. There will be moments where brief scrambling is required, but generally, the trail is in good condition along this ridge. At about 11,050 feet, the trail disappears into the rocky ridge, and the scrambling begins. This is an excellent place to either stash or pack up your trekking poles if you brought them. **Gloves and a helmet are highly recommended for this section.**

Author's Note
The Diamond Peak ridge is lesser known than its famous counterpart, Chicken Out Ridge of Borah Peak, but those who climb it will find a ridge substantially longer, more intense, and for some, more thrilling than Chicken Out. I recommend not starting with Diamond Peak if you are new to Class 3 climbing. For new hikers, the cliffs may be overwhelming.

Hikers shortly before the scramble on Diamond Peak.

The route up the ridge climbs around 1,100 feet in 0.6 miles on crumbling rock. The climbing is very much Class 3, though if you go off-course, you could find yourself in Class 4 or even Class 5 terrain. In general, hang on top of or to the right of the spine. Avoid going too low to the right, as staying higher on the ridge keeps you out of rockfall danger and away from unnecessary scree chutes. It's worth noting that there isn't any point during this lower section to ever be on the left (south), vertically exposed side of the ridge.

> **Author's Note**
> About midway up the ridge, you will come across an avoidable rock wall. Look for the large rock pile near the wall, and follow the small trail below the wall to the right. This will loop you around the cliff and back onto the route. Work your way back onto the ridge from there.

Don't climb this rock wall! Go shortly past it and make a left.

The Riddler as viewed from Diamond Peak.

Hikers near the summit of Diamond Peak. The difficulty decreases near the top.

After several more moderate climbing sections, you will reach the top of the spine, where it flattens out temporarily (11,730ft). You are close to the summit here. From this flat reprieve, continue west. The trail does hang left in a few instances, so don't be afraid to follow it. Make sure to get back up onto the spine whenever you can though.

Once the route turns left (southwest), it becomes much more manageable. The remaining 200 vertical feet give you a chance to finally take in the view as you make your way to the summit. On the summit, you get an excellent view of Bell Peak to the northwest, The Riddler to the south, and a great view of the Lost River Range to the west on clear days.

A hiker descending one of the many ridge scrambles on Diamond Peak.

Diamond Peak from the approach drive.

Elevation Profile

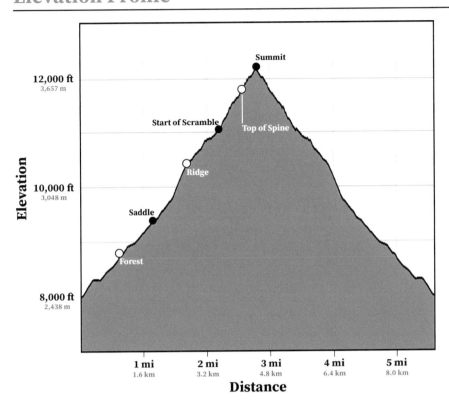

GPS Waypoints

Trailhead - 7,980 ft
N44° 08.881' W113° 02.258'

Forest - 8,740 ft
N44° 08.633' W113° 02.896'

Saddle - 9,370 ft
N44° 08.516' W113° 03.487'

Ridge - 10,385 ft
N44° 08.562' W113° 04.066'

Start of Scramble - 11,050 ft
N44° 08.719' W113° 04.490'

Top of Spine - 11,730 ft
N44° 08.615' W113° 04.810'

Summit - 12,197 ft
N44° 08.487' W113° 04.964'

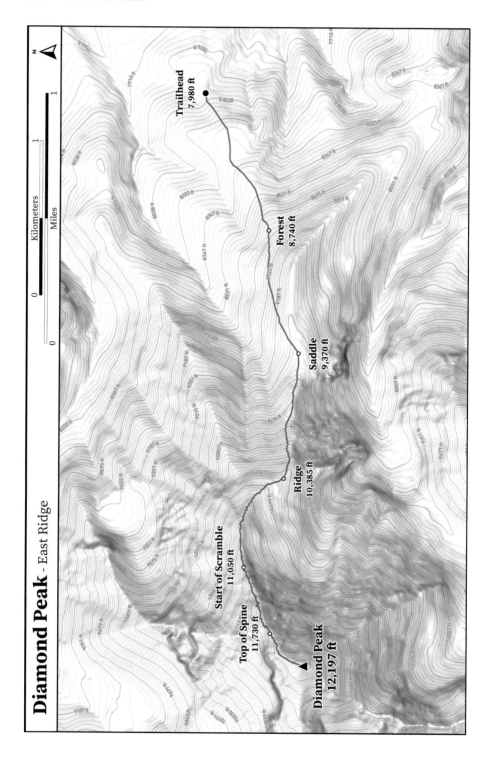

Diamond Peak - East Ridge

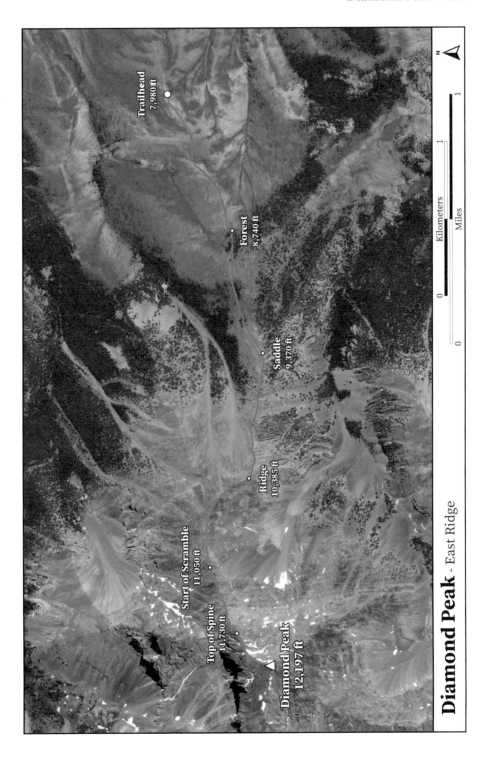

Diamond Peak - East Ridge

Trailhead
7,980 ft

Forest
8,740 ft

Saddle
9,370 ft

Ridge
10,385 ft

Start of Scramble
11,050 ft

Top of Spine
11,730 ft

Diamond Peak
12,197 ft

N

Kilometers

Miles

0   1

0   1

Glossary

4WD/AWD: Four-wheel drive / all-wheel drive

Alpine: The terrain above the tree line

Alpine Start: Beginning a climb at a very early hour

Altimeter: An instrument used to determine altitude

Altitude Sickness: A condition where lower oxygen pressure at high altitude causes physical distress

AMS: Acute Mountain Sickness, a form of altitude sickness

Anchor: A device used to connect a climber to another object, typically something to keep someone attached to a rock wall

Approach: The route to the base of the climb

Avalanche: A mass of debris, typically snow sliding down a mountain

Bail: Giving up on a climb

Barometer: An instrument used to measure changes in air pressure

Basin: An area with higher sides surrounding a low point, similar to a bowl

Beta: Useful information about a route

Bivy: Temporary and very portable shelter. Short for bivouac

Bottleneck: A narrow section of a route that can slow movement

Bushwhacking: Navigating terrain without an established path

Cairn: A distinct stack of rocks made by fellow climbers to mark a route

Chute: A steep narrow gully

Cirque: A half-open bowl formed by glacial erosion

Class Rating: The difficulty rating of a hike. See also Yosemite Decimal System

Cliff Out: When a hiker roams off-trail and becomes stuck in technical terrain

Contour Line: A line on a contour map that indicates an elevation

COR: Chicken Out Ridge, a notorious ridge on Borah Peak

Crampons: Metal attachments for boots that give traction on snow and ice. Typically used on glaciers and ice fields

Crux: The most challenging section of a climb

Deadfall: Fallen trees

Downclimb: Descending a route

Elevation Profile: A two-dimensional view of a landscape, showing distance and height

Exposure: Terrain where a fall could result in injury or death based on the steepness and height

Frostbite: Damage to the skin and underlying tissue due to exposure to cold and freezing

Glacier: A large mass of ice moving down a slope or spreading outward

Glissade: A method of sliding down a steep slope

GPS: Global Positioning System; a satellite-based navigation system

GPX: A file type containing geographic data used by GPS units

Gully: A narrow steep-sided ravine

HACE: High Altitude Cerebral Edema; excess fluid on the brain resulting in swelling

HAPE: High Altitude Pulmonary Edema; excess fluid accumulation in or on the lungs

Headwall: Terrain that steepens dramatically compared to everything preceding it

Hypothermia: When your body loses heat faster than it can produce it

Hypoxia: Unusually low or deficient oxygen in your body tissues

Ice Cleats: Small chains and spikes that are slipped over footwear to provide traction

Kit: A set of equipment

Ledge: A narrow and horizontal surface extending from a rock wall

Microspikes: Small chains that are slipped over footwear to provide traction

Mountaineer: A person who climbs mountains

Pass: A gap in terrain, such as a low point on a mountain ridge or saddle

Prominence: The height of a mountain relative to the lowest contour line encircling the mountain that does not have a higher summit within it

Ridge: A long and narrow crest of a mountain or hill

Rock Tower: A unique cliff or large rock formation

Rotten Rock: Rock that shifts or breaks apart easily

Saddle: The lowest point of a ridge connecting two mountains

Scree: Small rock fragments on the side or base of a mountain

Screebowl: A steep gully filled with scree

Sideflash: When lightning strikes one object, and then moves to a different object

Snow Bridge: Snow used as a path with steep sides alongside it

Spine: The top of a sharp ridge with defined sides

Summit: The highest point on a mountain

Super Gully: A large and steep gully found on Lost River Peak

Talus: Medium rock fragments on the side or base of a mountain

Technical: In climbing, when specific gear is needed to continue

Topo: A topographic map that shows elevation using contour lines

Traverse: A relatively horizontal section of a hike

Twelver: In Idaho, a 12,000-foot mountain
Ultra-Prominent: A mountain with over 4,900ft of topographic prominence
Upper Mountain: A term used to describe the exposed upper portion of a mountain, typically above the tree line
U-Valley: A glacially carved valley with the valley bottom and sides forming a "U" shape
Yosemite Decimal System: A specific climbing rating system to rate the difficulty of hikes and climbs. Ranges from Class 1 to Class 5

Contact Information

U.S Forest Service

Salmon-Challis National Forest
Forest Supervisor's Office
1206 S. Challis Street
Salmon, ID 83467
208-756-5100
https://www.fs.usda.gov/scnf

Sawtooth National Recreation Area (Sawtooth NRA)
5 North Fork Canyon Road
Ketchum, ID 83340
208-727-5000
https://www.fs.usda.gov/sawtooth

Caribou-Targhee National Forest
1405 Hollipark Drive
Idaho Falls, ID 83401
208-557-5900
https://www.fs.usda.gov/ctnf

Bureau of Land Management

Idaho State Office
1387 South Vinnell Way
Boise, ID 83709
208-373-4000
https://www.blm.gov/idaho

Mountain List

Mountain Name	Elevation	Prominence	Range	Page Number
Borah Peak	12,662 feet	5,982 feet	Lost River Range	49
Leatherman Peak	12,228 feet	1,667 feet	Lost River Range	77, 87
Mount Church	12,200 feet	919 feet	Lost River Range	99
Diamond Peak	12,197 feet	5,377 feet	Lemhi Range	141
Mount Breitenbach	12,140 feet	620 feet	Lost River Range	117
Lost River Peak	12,078 feet	678 feet	Lost River Range	129
Mount Idaho	12,065 feet	1,066 feet	Lost River Range	65
Donaldson Peak	12,023 feet	302 feet	Lost River Range	99
Hyndman Peak	12,009 feet	4,810 feet	Pioneer Mountains	35

Suggested Readings

Idaho: A Climbing Guide by Tom Lopez. An extensive and well-researched guide that is necessary reading for any Idaho climber.

Trails of Eastern Idaho by Margaret Fuller and Jerry Painter. A collection of Eastern Idaho trails, including the Twelvers.

The Mountaineer Handbook by Craig Connally. For those looking to expand their climbing abilities beyond day hiking into more advanced technical climbs.

Annotated Bibliography

AP. "Idaho's Highest Mountain To Be Called 'Borah Peak.'" *The Lewiston Morning Tribune*, February 12, 1934.

Connally, Craig. *The Mountaineering Handbook: Modern Tools and Techniques That Will Take You to the Top.* New York: McGraw-Hill, 2004.

"Hypothermia|Winter Weather." Centers for Disease Control and Prevention. Centers for Disease Control and Prevention, February 8, 2019. https://www.cdc.gov/disasters/winter/staysafe/hypothermia.html.

Lopez, Tom. *Idaho, a Climbing Guide: Climbs, Scrambles, and Hikes.* Seattle, WA: Mountaineers, 2000.

Rees, John E. *Idaho Chronology, Nomenclature, Bibliography.* W.B. Conkey Company, 1918.

Robbins, Dan. Idaho 12ers Home Page. https://idahosummits.com/over12/over12.htm.

Staff, KTVB. "Idaho's Only Glacier Formally Recognized by USGS." ktvb.com. KTVB, February 26, 2021. https://www.ktvb.com/article/news/local/idaho/idahos-only-glacier-usgs-mount-borah/277-e89a83bf-393d-4763-a299-6ce-9cdccc5ed.

United States Department of Agriculture. "The Day The Earth Shook." Oct. 1998.

"Warning Signs and Symptoms of Heat-Related Illness." Centers for Disease Control and Prevention. Centers for Disease Control and Prevention, September 1, 2017. https://www.cdc.gov/disasters/extremeheat/warning.html.

Merriam Lake from the summit of Mount Idaho.

Pocatello Trail Guide

Hiking, Biking, and Cross-Country Skiing Over 300 Miles of Trails Around The Gate City

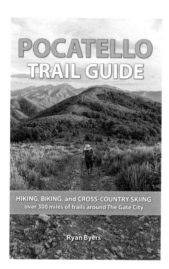

› Descriptions of routes ranging from family friendly trails all the way to summit hikes.

› Detailed directions to each trailhead.

› Quick Facts for each hike including distance, elevation gain, difficulty, and canine compatibility.

› Author-recommended Best Hikes and Best Rides, such as Best Wildflower Hikes and Best Hikes with Views.

Pocatello Trail Guide is the ultimate resource for anyone looking to explore Pocatello's many trails. Whether you're interested in the scenic river walks along the Portneuf Greenway or the forested paths of the Caribou-Targhee National Forest, this book provides hikers, mountain bikers, trail runners, and cross-country skiers with a comprehensive guide to accessing the numerous outdoor opportunities around The Gate City.

Available on Amazon and pocatellotrailguide.com

Lost River Publishing LLC   lostriverpublishing.com

About The Author

Ryan Byers is an avid outdoorsman who has been climbing and hiking in the Idaho wilderness since childhood. He received his B.S. from the University of Idaho and his MBA from Idaho State University. An accomplished endurance athlete, his love of peak bagging has led him across the United States and internationally to collect such notable summits as Pico de Orizaba, Iztaccihuatl, Mt. Rainier, and Gannett Peak. He is currently a videographer and writer.

Made in the USA
Columbia, SC
19 August 2024

40232577R00091